The
John F. Kennedy
Assassination
The Shooting That Shook America

By Joseph Stanley

Portions of this book originally appeared in
The John F. Kennedy Assassination by Stuart A. Kallen.

LUCENT
P R E S S

Published in 2018 by
Lucent Press, an Imprint of Greenhaven Publishing, LLC
353 3rd Avenue
Suite 255
New York, NY 10010

Designer: Deanna Paternostro
Editor: Siyavush Saidian

Cataloging-in-Publication Data

Names: Stanley, Joseph.
Title: The John F. Kennedy assassination: the shooting that shook America / Joseph Stanley.
Description: New York : Lucent Press, 2018. | Series: Crime scene investigations | Includes index.
Identifiers: ISBN 9781534560871 (library bound) | ISBN 9781534560888 (ebook)
Subjects: LCSH: Kennedy, John F. (John Fitzgerald), 1917-1963–Assassination–Juvenile literature.
Classification: LCC E842.Z9 S73 2017 | DDC 973.922092–dc23

Printed in the United States of America

CPSIA compliance information: Batch #BS17KL: For further information contact Greenhaven Publishing LLC, New York, New York at 1-844-317-7404.

Please visit our website, www.greenhavenpublishing.com. For a free color catalog of all our
high-quality books, call toll free 1-844-317-7404 or fax 1-844-317-7405.

Contents

Foreword

For decades, popular television programs and movies have depicted the life and work of police officers, detectives, and crime scene investigators. Many of these shows and films portray forensic scientists as the brains responsible for cracking cases and bringing criminals to justice. Undoubtedly, these crime scene analysts are an important part in the process of crime solving. With modern technology and advances in forensic analysis, these highly trained experts are a crucial component of law enforcement systems all across the world.

Police officers and detectives are also integral members of the law enforcement team. They are the ones who respond to 911 calls about crime, collect physical evidence, and use their high level of training to identify suspects and culprits. They work right alongside forensic investigators to figure out the mysteries behind why a crime is committed, and the entire team cooperates to gather enough evidence to convict someone in a court of law.

Ever since the first laws were recorded, crime scene investigation has been handled in roughly the same way. An authority is informed that a crime has been committed; someone looks around the crime scene and interviews potential witnesses; suspects are identified based on evidence and testimony; and, finally, someone is formally accused of committing a crime. This basic plan is generally effective, and criminals are often caught and brought to justice. Throughout history, however, certain limitations have sometimes prevented authorities from finding out who was responsible for a crime.

There are many reasons why a crime goes unsolved: Maybe a dead body was found too late, evidence was tampered with, or witnesses lied. Sometimes, even the greatest technology of the age is simply not good enough to process and analyze the evidence at a crime scene. In the United States during the 20th century, for example, the person responsible for the infamous Zodiac killings was never found, despite the earnest efforts of hundreds of policemen, detectives, and forensic analysts.

In modern times, science and technology are integral to the investigative process. From DNA analysis to high-definition surveillance video, it has become much more difficult to commit a crime and get away with it. Using advanced computers and immense databases, microscopic skin cells from a crime scene can be collected and then analyzed by a forensic scientist, leading detectives to the home of the culprit of a crime. Dozens of people work behind the scenes of criminal investigations to figure out the unique and complex elements of a crime. Although this process is still time-consuming and complicated, technology is constantly improving and adapting to the needs of police forces worldwide.

This series is designed to help young readers understand the systems in place to allow forensic professionals to do their jobs. Covering a wide range of topics, from the assassination of President John F. Kennedy to 21st-century cybercriminals, these titles describe in detail the ways in which technology and criminal investigations have evolved over more than 50 years. They cite eyewitnesses and experts in order to give a detailed and nuanced picture of the difficult task of rooting out criminals. Although television shows and movies add drama to the crime scene investigation process, these real-life stories have enough drama on their own. This series sticks to the facts surrounding some of the highest-profile criminal cases of the modern era and the people who work to solve them and other crimes every day.

Introduction
Still a Mystery

For the United States, the 1960s were a turbulent period. There were racial tensions between black and white Americans, the fight against Communism was turning neighbor against neighbor, and the Vietnam War was raging overseas. When John Fitzgerald Kennedy, commonly referred to as JFK, won the presidential election in 1960, everyone had high hopes that he would be the fresh, young leader the country needed to find its way through a difficult decade. For a time, he was.

After peacefully resolving several disputes with Cuba and the Soviet Union and making a series of highly motivational speeches around the world, millions of Americans saw JFK as a leader to believe in. However, on November 22, 1963, just two years after taking office, he was assassinated in Dallas, Texas, while riding in an open-top car in front of a large crowd. There is little evidence of the crime itself; only amateur photographs and video exist as a record of the murder. Despite the challenge of the case, law enforcement officials quickly tracked down one prime suspect: Lee Harvey Oswald.

Before the truth could come out in court, however, a man named Jack Ruby murdered Oswald out of revenge. With little evidence to use and a dead suspect, investigators had a difficult time piecing together the facts of the crime. JFK had a number of enemies who may have wanted him dead, including influential crime bosses, Russian spies, and even some members of the Central Intelligence Agency (CIA). Thousands of trained experts have tried to sort out the complex web of motives that surround the case, but the full story may never be known.

Broken Evidence

President Kennedy was killed in an era before the widespread use of digital cameras, cell phones, and 24-hour news coverage. In addition, crime scene

At 43, John F. Kennedy was the youngest president-elect in history when he won the election in 1960. He promised to bring stability to the country.

investigators did not have the forensic science tools that they have today. Though hundreds of people witnessed the murder, no one had a cell phone to record it. Police did not have powerful computers to match fingerprints, analyze evidence, or study DNA, even if they had some kind of hard evidence to examine. Moreover, many aspects of the Kennedy murder investigation were mishandled by the Dallas Police Department (DPD) and Federal Bureau of Investigation (FBI).

Conspiracy theorists—people who think the assassination was part of a large, international plot instead of the actions of just Lee Harvey Oswald—believe evidence was intentionally lost, manipulated, or even fabricated to frame Oswald or to cover

Though Dealey Plaza, shown here on the day of the assassination, had hundreds of potential eyewitnesses, the details of the murder are still widely debated.

up the existence of co-conspirators. Others argue that there was no precedent for a modern presidential assassination, and investigators were simply overwhelmed. The crime scene was large, it was filled with people, and there are major national security consequences when a president is murdered. In addition, investigators were concerned about the privacy of the Kennedy family. Not only were they treated like royalty by the press and public, but they had also just lost a husband, father, and leader.

A Doubtful Public

Because of all the confusion surrounding the case and the way the investigation was handled, millions of Americans started to doubt the official government story that Oswald was an assassin acting alone. In the years that followed, professional and amateur investigators combed through every bit of evidence surrounding the assassination. They analyzed many aspects surrounding the alleged murder weapon, including the bullets, the fingerprints on the rifle, and more. Audio and photographic forensic scientists studied a scratchy tape from a police radio and the amateur films that captured the president being shot. Forensic doctors studied the Kennedy autopsy along with materials that were preserved in the National Archives. Some used forensic psychology to study Oswald to determine his motivations. The truth, however, has remained elusive. Despite the decades of study and thousands of books written about the event, there are still questions about whether or not Oswald really killed JFK, if he acted alone, or whether he was involved in a larger conspiracy.

The harsh reality of crime scene investigation is that forensic evidence is often open to interpretation. In courtroom testimony, experts argue over the validity of fingerprints, firearm evidence, and autopsy findings. Even the accuracy of DNA evidence has been called into question in recent years. It is little wonder that the mishandled Kennedy investigation, with its major political implications, is still the subject of argument among both experts and amateur investigators. As each year passes, hopes dim that the mystery of the president's murder will ever be definitively solved.

Chapter One

Assassinating Trust

When President John F. Kennedy was assassinated in 1963, the nation changed forever. The barrage of bullets lasted roughly six seconds, but that was all it took to permanently transform the face of politics in the United States. The death of JFK and the subsequent investigation, which has been thoroughly criticized for its secretiveness and confusion, caused millions of people to lose faith in the government. According to polls, less than half of Americans believe that the official story of the assassination is true. Because of the mishandled evidence and unprofessional methods of investigation, however, no one has a clear view of what the truth is.

In 1963, forensic science was not well developed, and as a result, it was unreliable and untrusted. With today's technology, including high-definition video, DNA analysis, and other advanced investigative techniques, it is almost impossible to commit such a high-profile crime. Because evidence has been lost, contaminated, or, some people believe, manipulated, modern forensic analysts still cannot solve the JFK case. Professionals and amateurs alike have been publishing books and films that all propose different theories of the crime. Though some are more believable than others, none of them can be conclusively proved—or disproved. More than 50 years have passed since JFK's murder, and the American public still does not have a satisfactory explanation.

Riding in the Open

One of the great mysteries of the 20th century was set in motion at 11:38 a.m. on November 22, 1963, when Air Force One, the presidential plane, touched down at Love Field, an airport in Dallas. The 46-year-old president and his wife, Jacqueline Kennedy, fondly known as Jackie, came to Dallas to strengthen political support for Kennedy's second campaign for president in 1964. Texas was expected

Lyndon Baines Johnson, who was vice president under JFK, was a Texas native. He took over the office of president just two hours after JFK was assassinated in Dallas.

the party.

Kennedy was scheduled to give a speech to local business and civic leaders at a luncheon at the Dallas Trade Mart convention center. He was joined in the presidential limousine, a 1961 Lincoln four-door convertible, by First Lady Jackie Kennedy, Texas governor John Connally, and the governor's wife, Nellie. During the short drive to the Trade Mart, the Kennedys sat in the back seat, while Connally and his wife sat in front of them. Secret Service agent William Greer was behind the wheel.

Although the presidential limo had a clear, plastic "bubble top," which would have provided some protection to any passengers, it was not used on the day of the assassination. It was a bright and sunny day in Dallas, and the president believed that riding in an open car would encourage the image of unity he wanted to portray.

to play an important role in the next election. Kennedy's vice president, Lyndon B. Johnson, was a popular Texas native, but two major Texas politicians were in the middle of a feud. Because they were both Democrats, as was JFK, the president wanted to tour Dallas with the two men to show unity within

The presidential limousine is shown here moments before the assassination took place. Though riding without the top allowed the group to connect with the crowds in Dealey Plaza, it proved to be a fatal choice.

Love and Hate in Dallas

JFK was extremely popular across most of the United States, but Dallas was not a town that was entirely friendly toward Kennedy. Some residents harshly criticized JFK for his support of racial integration, a ban on nuclear testing, and diplomatic negotiations with the Soviet Union and other Communist governments. Before the president arrived in Dallas, a number of residents wished he would not come.

In fact, on the day Kennedy arrived, a group called the America-thinking

Citizens of Dallas placed an advertisement in a local paper that aggressively criticized the president and accused him of being "soft on Communists ... and ultra-leftists in America."[1] In the weeks leading up to his visit, leaflets were circulated throughout Dallas that showed President Kennedy, with a caption that read "Wanted For Treason: This Man Is Wanted for Treasonous Activities Against the United States."[2]

Despite the negative political atmosphere, the streets were lined with supportive crowds as Kennedy's limousine headed through downtown Dallas. The presidential motorcade turned right from Main Street onto Houston Street, drove one block, then made a sharp left onto Elm Street. In order to make this final turn, the motorcade was forced to slow down to 11 miles (18 km) per hour. Security experts have pointed out that this speed was a safety hazard, because it made the president an easier target.

The limousine maintained this slow speed as it coasted down the street in front of the seven-story Texas School Book Depository, a book distribution warehouse. All four of the car's passengers smiled and waved at the enthusiastic crowds. Mrs. Connally turned to the president and said, "Mr. President, you can't say Dallas doesn't love you." Kennedy replied, "That's obvious."[3]

Once past the Book Depository, the motorcade approached a small grassy area called Dealey Plaza. It was named after George Bannerman Dealey, a major executive involved with the *Dallas Morning News*. This small park is bordered on the west by a large railroad bridge. Around this time, a few cars ahead of the presidential limousine,

Dealey Plaza, shown here, had a lot of places for an assassin to hide. Many people believe a second shooter was on the grassy knoll in the lower right of this picture.

Too Many Enemies

When John F. Kennedy arrived in Dallas on November 22, 1963, the Secret Service was worried about the president's safety. Kennedy had made many political and social enemies in his first two years in office.

Some of his enemies can be traced back to events that took place months before his 1960 election. In January 1959, Communist revolutionary Fidel Castro overthrew the Cuban government in a military coup, deposing an oppressive dictator who was friendly to the United States. In the aftermath, Castro shut down hundreds of casinos, nightclubs, and other operations that had been making money for organized criminal gangs.

Within the United States, CIA officials made plans to oust Castro because they feared he would allow the Soviet Union to establish military bases on the island, which is just 90 miles (145 km) from Florida. The CIA trained 1,500 Cuban exiles to invade Cuba in a southwest region called the Bay of Pigs. They were to be aided by fighter pilots, who would drop bombs on Cuban military targets. This combined force was ready to attack Castro in April 1961, several months after Kennedy was inaugurated.

The soldiers, however, were quickly and decisively defeated once they reached Cuba. Many were taken hostage and ransomed back to the United States for millions of dollars. JFK's top advisers told him that he was given bad information from the CIA in an attempt to manipulate him. Angry and betrayed, he reportedly pledged to dissolve the CIA. The Bay of Pigs invasion made Kennedy three major enemies at once. Conspiracy researchers believe any number of people associated with anti-Castro Cubans, pro-Castro Cubans, or the CIA itself could have participated in JFK's assassination.

Secret Service agent Winston Lawson radioed ahead to the Trade Mart and said the motorcade would be arriving in five minutes.

To the president's right, a small hill, now famously known as the grassy knoll, rose at the back of Dealey Plaza. At the top of the grassy knoll, a picket fence extended from a passageway of columns called a colonnade. These slight barriers separated Dealey Plaza from a busy railroad yard and dirt parking lot.

Three Shots

Shortly after a large clock on top of the

By the Numbers

0

number of U.S. presidents who have used an open limousine since Kennedy's assassination

The Bay of Pigs incident led to the capture of hundreds of Cuban fighters. It was a permanent stain on Kennedy's record. Some conspiracy theorists believe that the CIA or Cuban government may have been involved in his assassination.

Book Depository changed to 12:30 p.m., the sound of gunfire filled the air. One researcher described the sequence of events that followed:

According to a Secret Service agent in the car, the President ... lurched in his seat, both hands clawing toward his throat ... Directly in front of the President, Governor Connally had heard one shot and was then hit himself. He screamed

... Then had come more gunfire. The President had fallen violently backward and to his left ... From the front seat the Governor's wife heard the President's wife exclaim, "Jack ... they've killed my husband." Then: "I have his brains in my hand." This last Mrs. Kennedy repeated time and time again.[4]

During the shooting, Governor Connally sustained wounds in his back, right chest, right wrist, and left thigh. As the bullets rained down, Secret Service agent Clint Hill, who had been running behind the car, jumped on the bumper of the limousine and crawled up on the trunk to block the president and Mrs. Kennedy from further shots.

The attack lasted roughly six seconds. As the sound of gunfire stopped echoing throughout Dealey Plaza, Greer accelerated the presidential limousine, driving to Parkland Memorial Hospital. It was there that doctors worked in vain to save the president's life. Their efforts failed, and Kennedy was pronounced dead at 1:00 p.m. Although Governor Connally was badly wounded, he eventually recovered from his injuries.

Immediate Investigation

As JFK's limousine sped off, there was chaos in Dealey Plaza. Dozens of people had thrown themselves to the ground during the shooting, and police and federal agents were running around frantically. Some witnesses thought the shots came from behind the picket fence on the grassy knoll; others pointed to the large railroad bridge to the west. Most people claimed that they heard the shots come from the Book Depository. Dallas motorcycle patrolman Marrion Baker had seen startled pigeons flying off the roof of the Book Depository as the gunshots rang out. He pulled out his gun and ran into the building, searching for

anyone suspicious.

Baker and building supervisor Roy Truly ran up the stairs in the building to the second-floor lunchroom. There, they encountered Lee Harvey Oswald, who had worked at the Book Depository for several months. Truly later recalled, "Oswald didn't seem to be excited or overly afraid."[5] Because of Oswald's calm demeanor, Officer Baker dismissed him as a suspect and moved on in his search for the assassin. Several minutes later, Oswald casually walked out of the Book Depository and boarded a city bus.

Other officers were called to the scene to search the sixth floor of the Book Depository. Captain John Will Fritz, chief of the homicide and robbery bureau of the Dallas Police Department, arrived to take control of the investigation. Authorities found three spent bullet cartridges in the southeast corner of the sixth floor, an area now known as the sniper's nest. The shell casings lay near a half-opened window that overlooked Elm Street and the motorcade route. Police searching the northwest corner of the sixth floor also found a rifle with a telescopic sight stashed between two pallets piled with cartons of books.

A Prime Suspect

As police searched the Book Depository for the gunman, Oswald's bus moved slowly through the heavy traffic that had been caused by the day's events.

The Texas School Book Depository building, shown here, was at the center of the controversy surrounding the JFK assassination. Lee Harvey Oswald, the alleged killer, had been working there shortly before the murder.

Eventually, Oswald got off the bus and hailed a cab to take him to the boarding house where he lived.

About 30 minutes after the assassination, Oswald entered his rented room, changed his shirt, and grabbed a Smith & Wesson .38-caliber revolver. Although there were no witnesses, police say Oswald left his house shortly after 1:00 p.m. and walked about a mile. Like many components of the JFK assassination, Oswald's actions after this time are debated.

Authorities say that Dallas police officer J.D. Tippit heard a series of announcements on his police radio between 12:45 and 1:00 that described the assassin. The suspected killer had been described as a thin, 30-year-old white male around 5 feet, 10 inches (1.8 m) tall and weighing about 165 pounds (75 kg). The officer saw Oswald walking down the street shortly after 1:00 and believed he fit that description. Tippet stopped Oswald to question him. The officer exited his car and walked around the front of the vehicle to talk to him. Almost immediately, Oswald allegedly pulled out his gun and shot Tippit four times, killing him. There were more than 10 people in the vicinity who witnessed the killing or saw the shooter shortly after.

Witnesses then saw Oswald running into a nearby movie house, the Texas Theatre, where he snuck in without paying. When reports of Tippit's shooting were broadcast over the police radio, more than 10 police officers converged on the movie house. Officers found Oswald sitting in the nearly empty theater. When one of the officers approached, Oswald punched him in the face. During the short scuffle that ensued, Oswald allegedly tried to shoot the officers, but the gun did not fire. He was finally overpowered by several police officers.

As they led the suspect through the theater lobby, Oswald yelled, "I want my lawyer. I know my rights. Typical police brutality. Why are you doing this to me?"[6] Oswald was transported to Dallas police headquarters. During the ride to the station, officers observed that Oswald was calm and collected, showing no emotion while denying any involvement in the Tippit shooting.

Irregularities

Around 2:00 p.m., the patrol car with Oswald pulled into the basement of Dallas police headquarters. Dozens of reporters and photographers were gathered to see the suspect. An officer asked Oswald if he wanted a jacket over his head to hide his identity from the press. Oswald answered, "Why should I cover my face? I haven't done anything to be ashamed of."[7] When Oswald was taken upstairs to be booked, the arresting officers only told detectives they captured the man who killed Officer Tippit. Upon searching the suspect's wallet, police found two forms of identification: one identifying the man as Lee Oswald, the other identifying him as Alek James Hidell. Investigators later discovered that A.J. Hidell was a fake name he sometimes used.

In the hour before Oswald's arrest, Captain Fritz had been notified by Roy Truly that Oswald was missing from the Texas School Book Despository. Fritz believed that Oswald, an employee of the building, was the main suspect in the Kennedy assassination. When Fritz arrived at DPD headquarters that afternoon, he mentioned the name of the missing employee—and discovered that Oswald had already been arrested and was in the interrogation room. Meanwhile, just after 2:30 p.m., little more than three hours after the Kennedys landed in Dallas, vice president Lyndon Johnson was sworn in as president of the United States. Standing next to him, a grief-stricken Jackie Kennedy looked on, her Chanel suit and white gloves stained with her husband's blood.

By later that afternoon, the third floor of police headquarters was in chaos. Officers were transferring Oswald to the building's basement. There, he was placed in a police lineup, where a woman who had witnessed Tippit's murder from several blocks away identified Oswald as the killer. Oswald, who had not yet been charged with Kennedy's murder, seemed surprised by the reception. When asked if he killed the president, he said that no one had charged him with that yet, and in fact, it was the first time he had heard of such a charge. When he realized what was happening, he told reporters he was being set up to take the blame for the Kennedy assassination, yelling "I'm just a patsy!"[8] A patsy is someone who is used or manipulated by someone else to commit a crime.

Oswald was led to Captain Fritz's office, where he underwent intense questioning by city, state, and federal authorities. Captain Fritz took notes during

After Oswald was arrested, police found out that he had been using several fake identities, such as this one, for a few years. He used the name Alek Hidell to purchase the alleged murder weapon.

Interrogation Procedure

Investigators who interview criminal suspects must combine their expert training, psychological analysis, and quick, creative thinking to get people to talk. For many years, law enforcement agencies across America used the Reid interrogation model, which encouraged investigators to accuse suspects and get them to confess. Critics have argued that the Reid method, however, encourages innocent people to confess to crimes they did not commit. New procedures have been introduced in recent years, and one is called the PEACE model, which breaks down to mean:

1. *Preparation and Planning. Interviewers should create a written interview plan … Interviewers should consider characteristics of the [suspect] that could be relevant to the plan …*

2. *Engage and Explain. The interviewers should engage the individual … The interviewers should explain the reasons for the interview … Interviewers should encourage the individual to state anything they believe is relevant.*

3. *Account. The interviewers should use appropriate questions and active listening to obtain the [suspect's] account of events. Questions should be short and [easy to understand] …*

4. *Closure … Avoid an abrupt end to the interview … the interviewers should summarize the person's account of events, allowing the person to make clarifications and ask questions.*

5. *Evaluate. The interviewers should evaluate the interview to … assess how the [suspect's] account fits in with the investigation … [and] determine if further action is needed.[1]*

1. James Orlando, "Interrogation Techniques." OLR Research Report. www.cga.ct.gov/2014/rpt/2014-R-0071.htm.

his initial interviews, but no known notes, tape recordings, or films were made during the subsequent 12 hours of FBI interrogation. The lack of an official transcript is a point of concern for conspiracy theorists. Jim Garrison, an experienced attorney, wrote,

The Dallas Police Department … conducted a highly irregular inquiry. For example, after his arrest Lee Harvey Oswald was questioned while in the custody of Captain Will Fritz, head of the Dallas Police Homicide Division. As a prosecutor, I knew that recording

of such questioning is routine even in minor felony cases. Yet ... the alleged murderer of the President of the United States had been questioned for a total of 12 hours without any taping or shorthand notes ... Nor was any attorney present. The absence of any record of the interrogation of Oswald revealed a disregard for basic constitutional rights ... This could not be mere sloppiness, I realized. A police officer of 30 years' experience like Captain Fritz had to be aware that anything Oswald said under such circumstances would be inadmissible in any subsequent trial.[9]

A government investigation of the case later blamed the unusual nature of the interrogation on the general state of chaos and confusion in the station at the time. The interrogation room itself was packed with Secret Service agents, FBI agents, and Dallas police officers. Moreover, all these law enforcement officials had just been around the death of President Kennedy. It was a hectic and emotionally difficult environment.

A Strong Will

The next day, Saturday, November 23, was a day of sadness for a shocked nation. As millions mourned their fallen president, the FBI released dozens of facts concerning Oswald's somewhat strange background. He did not finish high school. After serving in the Marines from 1956 to 1959, he attempted to renounce his American citizenship and join the Soviet Union, where he lived for several years. He then returned to the United States in 1962. He spoke fluent Russian, a language he had picked up during his time in the Marines.

In the months before Kennedy's assassination, Oswald was arrested for handing out fliers in support of Communism on a street corner in New Orleans, Louisiana. In addition, a short time before the assassination, Oswald reportedly traveled to Mexico City, where he went to the Cuban consulate and indicated a serious desire to move to Cuba. These facts led investigating officers to conclude that Lee Harvey Oswald was a Communist whose political beliefs had inspired the murder of the president of the United States. Some suspected that Oswald might have even been working with spies from Cuba, the Soviet Union, or another organization.

Oswald never had the chance to publicly explain his actions. Two days after Kennedy's murder, on November 24, authorities decided to move the suspect from the city jail to the more secure county jail. At about 11:20 a.m., the handcuffed prisoner, surrounded by several police detectives, was led through the prisoner transfer area in the basement of the Dallas police headquarters

Tasked with the Truth

During murder trials, defense lawyers use forensic evidence and testimony from investigators, experts, and eyewitnesses to cast doubt on the defendant's guilt. If the accused person dies before being tried in court, then the case never goes to trial. Because he was murdered, Lee Harvey Oswald was never tried in a court of law to determine whether or not he killed President Kennedy. This is addressed in the foreword of the Warren Commission's report, which detailed the investigation of the assassination:

> *If Oswald had lived he could have had a trial by American standards of justice where he would have been able to exercise his full rights under the law. A judge and jury would have presumed him innocent until proven guilty beyond a reasonable doubt. He might have furnished information which could have affected the course of his trial ... There could have been an examination to determine whether he was sane ... The Commission has functioned neither as a court presiding over [a criminal trial] nor as a prosecutor determined to prove a case, but as a fact-finding agency committed to [learning] the truth.*[1]

1. President's Commission on the Assassination of President Kennedy, *Report of the President's Commission on the Assassination of President Kennedy*. Washington, DC: United States Government Printing Office, 1964, p. xiv. www.archives.gov/research/jfk/warren-commission-report/foreword.html.

toward a waiting armored car. The media was allowed in the general area, but the police had kept many details of the transfer a secret.

The transfer area was in an underground parking garage that was crowded with reporters and onlookers. Despite heavy security, Jack Ruby, a nightclub owner who allegedly had connections to organized crime, leapt out of the crowd and shot Oswald in the stomach with a .38-caliber revolver. Unlike Kennedy's assassination, this event was captured on live television, with dozens of cameras and direct

witnesses. Since ABC, CBS, and NBC, the three major television networks at the time, had suspended regular programming to broadcast the breaking news, millions of people witnessed the shooting live that Sunday morning.

After being shot, Oswald was conscious for a few moments. Sensing this might be the last chance to talk to the suspect, Detective Billy Combest tried to close the case:

> *I got right down on the floor with him, just literally on my hands and knees. And I asked him if he would*

ABOVE: Jack Ruby aims at Presidential assassin Lee Oswald in Dallas. BELOW: He shoots.
Stories begin on page 2; six full picture pages

Lee Harvey Oswald was never put on trial for the assassination of JFK because he was murdered himself—with millions of Americans watching.

Occupation: Secret Service Agent

Job Description:
U.S. Secret Service agents work under the supervision of the Department of Homeland Security. They serve a wide range of security functions, including: investigating financial crimes, such as counterfeiting, bank fraud, computer and telecommunications fraud, and money laundering; protecting the president, the vice president, and their immediate families; and protecting former presidents, their spouses, their children, and visiting heads of foreign governments.

Education:
Aspiring Secret Service agents must possess, at minimum, a bachelor's degree from an accredited college or university, or have at least one year of work experience in the criminal investigation or law enforcement fields.

Qualifications:
Secret Service applicants must be U.S. citizens who are at least 21 years of age and younger than 37. They must have a valid driver's license and excellent eyesight without glasses. Applicants must take rigorous written examinations, pass strenuous physical testing, and submit to a complete background investigation, which includes in-depth interviews, drug screening, a medical examination, and a polygraph examination (lie detector test).

Salary:
In 2014, the average starting salary for new Secret Service agents was $44,043.

like to make any confession, any statement in connection with the assassination of the President ... he responded to me by shaking his head [no] in a definitive manner ... He wasn't going to [talk] with me, he wasn't going to say anything.[10]

Oswald was taken to Parkland Memorial Hospital, where the same doctors who had tried to save President Kennedy now tried to save his accused assassin. Their efforts were again unsuccessful, and Oswald died at 1:07 p.m. He was buried in Dallas on November 25. On that same day, President John F. Kennedy was laid to rest in Arlington National Cemetery in Virginia.

A Long Mystery

In the days following the assassination, Oswald's ties to Cuba and the Soviet Union were widely publicized in the press. This led many Americans to conclude that their president had been murdered by an agent acting for an enemy country. If true, Kennedy's assassination was an act of war. During this era, known as the Cold War, the Soviet Union and the United States had thousands of nuclear missiles aimed at one another, ready to launch at a moment's notice. If JFK's murder ignited World War III, it would have likely led to the complete destruction of the human race.

In order to dispel rumors and fears, President Johnson quickly contacted Soviet leaders, who assured him they did not plot to kill Kennedy. To satisfy the American public that there was no conspiracy, Johnson issued Executive Order No. 11130 on November 29, 1963. This order created a presidential commission to investigate Kennedy's assassination. It was headed by Supreme Court chief justice Earl Warren and became known as the Warren Commission. Allen Dulles, who had recently resigned as CIA director under pressure by JFK, was one of the most controversial members of the Warren Commission because of his known dislike of the dead president. Other, less famous members of the Warren Commission included future president Gerald Ford and future senator Arlen Specter. None of the commission members had a history in criminal investigation, and they did not hire outside investigators. Instead, they relied on the findings of the FBI and CIA to draw their conclusions.

Answers proved to be difficult to come by. This prompted Warren to say, "We may never know the full story in our lifetime."[11] In addition, the commission was under pressure by President Johnson to produce a report quickly, before the upcoming presidential election in November 1964.

The Warren Commission operated entirely in secret and visited Dallas several times. It relied extensively on expert testimony regarding the evidence available at the time. On September 27, 1964, the commissioners released the *Report of the Warren Commission on the Assassination of President Kennedy*, commonly referred to as the Warren report. It included a huge quantity of evidence and expert testimony and an 888-page summary that concluded that Lee Harvey Oswald, acting alone, shot President Kennedy with a Mannlicher-Carcano rifle from a sixth-floor sniper's nest in the Texas School Book Depository. Oswald was himself murdered by Jack Ruby two days later. Ruby claimed that anger and sadness over JFK's death had caused him to aggressively lash out against Oswald, the accused murderer. The Warren report also concluded, "the Commission has found no evidence that either Lee Harvey Oswald or Jack Ruby was part of any conspiracy, domestic or foreign, to assassinate President Kennedy ... On the basis of the evidence before the Commission it concludes that Oswald acted alone."[12]

By the Numbers

4

number of U.S. presidents who have been assassinated

Uncertainty

As soon as the Warren report was released, most major newspapers and national magazines endorsed its conclusions. Most reported that the Warren Commission's investigation was thorough. Despite widespread media support, not everyone was convinced. Most prominent among doubters was Robert Kennedy, the president's brother and the attorney general of the United States. Though he never openly claimed that his brother's assassination was part of an international conspiracy, he also never fully endorsed the Warren report. In the years to come, thousands of medical, scientific, legal, and law enforcement researchers came to agree with

Robert Kennedy. They based this on inconsistencies they found in the report and on the panel's refusal to release documents and evidence for review by outside agencies.

The first published criticism of the Warren report hit bookstands in 1966. *Rush to Judgment*, written by attorney Mark Lane, argued against much of the evidence presented in the Warren report. Lane decided to write the book after his appeal to defend Oswald before the Warren Commission was rejected. The attorney believed Oswald was innocent and, although he was dead, he was entitled to legal representation before the Warren Commission. In rejecting Lane's request, Warren insisted that the panel was set up only to sort out and understand the facts of the case. It was not created to put Oswald on trial for a criminal offense.

Released two years after the Warren report, with the nation still recovering from the shock of JFK's death, *Rush to Judgment* was one of the best selling books of 1966. People were still deeply interested in the assassination of the widely respected president. In the following years, many more books were published that re-evaluated the evidence and raised questions about the Warren Commission's findings, continuing the mystery behind the president's murder.

Confusion and Conspiracies

When the Warren report was published in September 1964, most media outlets supported the conclusions that Oswald acted alone when he shot Kennedy. Although some reporters and editorial writers doubted the findings and publicized alternative conclusions, they were accused of being agitators, conspiracy theorists, and even enemies of the United States. Many of these people were criticized for simply trying to stir up fear across the country. Observers commented that most conspiracy theories were crafted to make America look weak or make foreign countries look strong. Though the event is more than 50 years old, neither side—believers of the Warren report and doubters—has been able to win a decisive victory. There are uncountable numbers of different theories about the Kennedy assassination, and none of them have been definitively proven.

Conflicting theories place the blame on suspects that include Mafia hit men; Secret Service, FBI, and CIA agents; and even President Lyndon Johnson. The various conspiracy theories were fueled by the government's refusal to release the documents and the forensic evidence used by the Warren Commission. Though independent investigators have since examined thousands of these documents and much of the forensic evidence, there are still no concrete conclusions. The secrecy of the 1960s left the American public wondering about the motives behind the murder of the young president, and the world has not been able to stop wondering well into the 21st century.

Chapter Two
Doctors and Mysteries

The November 22, 1963, assassination of President John F. Kennedy left the United States without a leader in uncertain times. Though the new president, Lyndon Johnson, had created the Warren Commission to research, investigate, and draw conclusions about the monumental case, the results did not make many people happy. Mainstream media sources expressed confidence in the Warren report, but eyewitnesses and experts were coming forward to cast doubt on its conclusions. By the mid-1960s, a large portion of Americans did not believe the conclusion that Lee Harvey Oswald had acted alone.

If they did not believe Oswald acted independently, that means he must have been part of a larger conspiracy. People pointed to Kennedy's feuds with the CIA, the FBI, organized crime bosses, and the Communist governments of Cuba and the Soviet Union and argued that any one of them could have pulled off an assassination. One of the ways people wanted to make this claim was by looking at the number of times JFK was shot, how the bullets entered his body, and the direction they came from. To find this out, investigators turned to forensic medical analysts.

Forensic medicine is used by specially trained doctors to determine the cause of death in criminal cases and gather the evidence to prove it. Modern forensic medicine allows doctors to trace the angle of a bullet entering a victim, analyze how that gunshot caused the death, and give other forensic examiners evidence to solve a crime. In the 1960s, however, this branch of science was not as advanced. The Warren Commission used testimony from the emergency room surgeons who tried to save JFK's life and the doctors who performed his autopsy to confirm their theory: He was shot by a lone gunman. However, some critics have argued that this evidence is inaccurate or incomplete.

Moreover, because Oswald did not live to stand trial, the forensic doctors did not have to assemble a thorough and complete conclusion of Kennedy's death. Forensic science is specifically used to gather evidence to use in court, but because the case never made it that far, their analysis was not extremely detailed. Conspiracy theorists have argued that because of this, there is not enough evidence to definitively say Oswald was the killer. Furthermore, some theorists believe that the evidence was actually manipulated and mishandled to specifically frame Oswald for a crime he did not commit.

From the ER

When President Kennedy was wheeled into the emergency operating room at Parkland Memorial Hospital a few minutes after he was shot, there was little hope the doctors could save him. A bullet had destroyed a huge portion of his skull and brain on the top and right side of his head. Despite his condition, Kennedy continued to breathe as the doctors and nurses struggled to save his life somehow.

Surgeon Charles A. Crenshaw was a resident physician at Parkland Hospital that day. Residency is a period of specialized training when a graduate of medical school practices under the supervision of an experienced doctor. In his three-year residency at Parkland, Crenshaw had treated gunshot victims before. He noted that a bullet had entered the president's neck and pierced his windpipe. In Crenshaw's recollection, the wound on the front of Kennedy's throat appeared smaller than the wound at the back. This would indicate, he argued, that the throat wound was made by a bullet that entered from the front. In addition, the doctor believed the bullet that struck the president's head also came from in front of the limousine and not from the Texas School Book Depository, which was located behind Kennedy at the time of the shooting. As Crenshaw explained,

I walked to the President's head to get a closer look. [One] portion of his brain appeared to be gone. It looked like a crater ... From the damage I saw, there was no doubt in my mind that the bullet had entered his head through the front ... The wound resembled a deep furrow in a freshly plowed field. Several years later when I viewed slow-motion films of the bullet striking the President, the physics of the head being thrown back provided final and complete confirmation of a frontal entry by the bullet.[13]

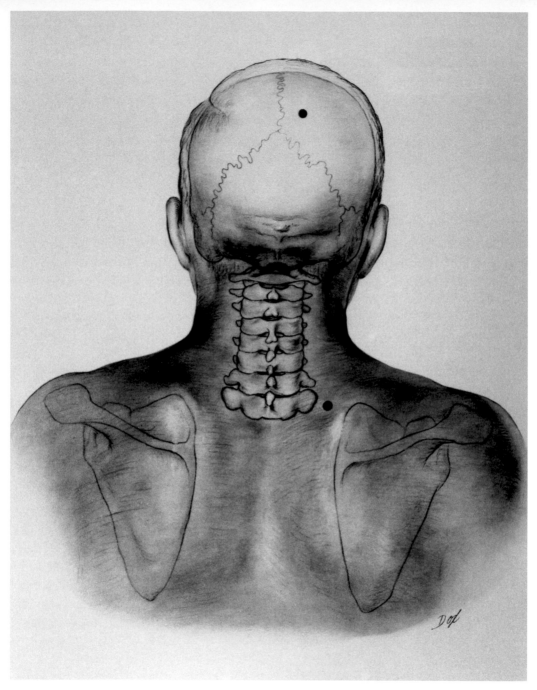

In this official drawing of Kennedy's wounds, the black dots indicate that the president was shot through the neck area and fatally through the head.

A Different Time

Before the rise of modern technology, medical records were difficult to keep track of—even for a president. When the mortally wounded JFK was brought to Parkland Memorial Hospital on November 22, 1963, doctors did not even know his blood type. Things have changed dramatically since then, especially for presidents. During his presidency, Barack Obama's limousine reportedly had a blood bank in the trunk, stocked with the appropriate blood in case it was needed. In his book on the Kennedy assassination, Dr. Charles A. Crenshaw discussed what health care was like in 1963 when he treated Kennedy after the shooting:

When John F. Kennedy came to Dallas [in 1963], health care was very different from what it is today, especially in the treatment of trauma-related injuries. Ambulances were hearses equipped with a single tank of oxygen, and there were no emergency technicians. Blood from African Americans was not allowed to be transfused into whites, and vice versa. Other hospitals in Dallas didn't want to treat trauma cases because they were a money-losing [job]. A hospital's entire annual budget for such care could be, and many times was, spent on a few patients. And there were no such programs as Medicare or Medicaid. Mostly, we were treating the poor and underprivileged. Given the choice, a person of any [wealth] would never have chosen to go to Parkland because of its reputation— that is, unless he was in need of trauma care, in which case Parkland Hospital substantially improved his chances for survival. Otherwise, the selection would have been a private hospital.[1]

1. Charles A. Crenshaw, *Trauma Room One: The JFK Medical Coverup Exposed.* New York, NY: Paraview, 2001, p. 25.

After studying the wound, the doctors in the emergency room concluded that there was no way to save the president. Even if he lived, it would have been in a vegetative state. After several more minutes of frantic effort to save Kennedy, the doctors gave up. One of the physicians turned to Jackie Kennedy, who had come into the emergency room. He said, "Your husband has sustained a fatal wound."[14]

By 1:00 p.m., the president was officially declared dead. A Catholic priest administered his last rites as he lay in the operating room. Before 2:00 p.m., the world learned of the president's passing when CBS anchor Walter Cronkite interrupted the soap opera *As the World Turns* to announce the news on national television.

After Death

Inside the hospital, two employees of the O'Neal Funeral Home wheeled a brass casket into the operating room. Kennedy's body had been cleaned and wrapped in white sheets. Crenshaw was the only doctor left in the room, and before he ordered the body removed, he reported that he took a last long look at the head wound before the casket was sealed and wheeled from the room on a gurney.

Later, Crenshaw noted his observations concerning the wounds sustained by the president. Although Ronald Jones and Robert McClelland, two more doctors who operated on JFK, testified before the Warren Commission, their observations about the exit wound at the back of Kennedy's skull were either ignored or overruled by other evidence. The Warren report stated that Kennedy was shot from behind, by Oswald, from the sixth floor of the Book Depository.

In the decades since the assassination, many medical experts have viewed the forensic evidence of Kennedy's wounds, including photographs, drawings, and autopsy reports, that was compiled in the hours and days after the assassination. These investigations have come to many different conclusions regarding the direction of the bullets. Some agree with the findings of the Warren report and explain that the head wound supports this conclusion. Others believe the conclusions of the Warren Commission are incorrect. They say the head wound is evidence that Kennedy was shot from the front.

Who Has Control?

At the time of Kennedy's death, there was no federal law that made assassinating a president illegal. Whoever had killed JFK was guilty of homicide, or murder, under Texas state law. In Texas, a homicide requires a justice of the peace to conduct an investigation about the circumstances of the murder. In Dallas County, the justice of the peace at the time was Theron Ward, who rushed to Parkland Memorial Hospital not long after doctors declared the president's death. Because the assassination of the president was technically not a federal crime, Texas law enforcement officials attempted to take control of the investigation.

Texas law mandated that before the body of any homicide victim can be transported, a thorough autopsy must be performed by a county medical examiner to determine the cause and circumstance of death. The Dallas County medical examiner was Dr. Earl F. Rose, but before he could perform the forensic autopsy operation as required by law, a power struggle began between Dallas law enforcement and the federal Secret Service.

In the aftermath of Kennedy's assassination, there was a power struggle between Dallas police and the federal Secret Service. Many have argued that the Secret Service's intervention caused confusion regarding the medical reports of JFK's death.

Rose had already issued instructions to prepare Kennedy for the autopsy. This was part of his legal duty, which also included gathering evidence during the examination of the president's clothes and, later, the scene of the crime. These investigations would help Rose establish how many bullets were fired and from which direction. However, by this time, the emergency room and hallways were filled with dozens of military officers, officials of the Kennedy administration, and Secret Service and FBI agents.

The Secret Service agents tried to take control of the situation and the president's body. One of the doctors politely explained that, under Texas law, Rose was required to conduct an autopsy before the body could be moved. The agents demanded that they be allowed to take custody of the president's corpse. Meanwhile, Rose had called Dallas district attorney Henry Wade for help, and Wade was instructing him to search the body for bullets and preserve them as evidence.

The federal authorities were not willing to comply with this request, as they wanted to start transporting the body back to Washington, D.C., immediately. This caused Rose to yell, "We can't release anything! A violent death requires [an autopsy]! There's a law here. We're going to enforce it."[15]

As Jackie Kennedy stood beside her husband's casket, about 40 men gathered around the casket, yelling and arguing about the president's body. Theron Ward soon arrived on the scene, and informed the crowd that it was his legal duty to order an autopsy. Some of the agents told Ward that it would not be right to force the First Lady and the president's staff to wait in Texas. After a brief struggle over the casket, the Secret Service took control of the president's remains. Experts in forensic medicine have widely criticized this turn of events. Standard procedure for homicide victims was not followed, which most likely destroyed or changed any evidence that could have been extracted by examining Kennedy's body. Moreover, because Texas law was not followed and an autopsy was not immediately performed, there have been continuous questions about the accuracy of later medical reports.

Spoiled Evidence

Kennedy's casket was loaded into a hearse and driven to the airport in Love Field by Secret Service agents. However, no one had prepared a forklift to load the large brass casket onto the plane. Because the agents wanted to depart as quickly as possible, they carried the coffin by hand. However, it was wider than the steps of the plane, and it took a clumsy effort to get the casket loaded onto the airplane. Once again, agents ignored proper procedure as they roughly moved the body of a pre-autopsy murder victim. Their actions may have altered important medical evidence.

Whose Brain Is It Anyway?

Questions about Kennedy's brain autopsy came to light in 1998 when the Assassinations Records Review Board released a number of records from the National Archives relating to Kennedy's murder. During the partial brain autopsy, a navy photographer took pictures of the procedure. However, some of the photographs in the National Archives appear to be inconsistent with the Dallas doctors' reports. Because of this uncertainty, Douglas Horne, chief analyst of military records for the Assassinations Records Review Board, concluded, "I am 90 to 95 percent certain that the photographs in the Archives are not of President Kennedy's brain. If they aren't, that can mean only one thing—that there has been a coverup of the medical evidence."[1]

1. Quoted George Lardner Jr., "Archive Photos Not of JFK's Brain, Concludes Aide to Review Board," *Washington Post*, November 10, 1998. www.washingtonpost.com/wp-srv/national/longterm/jfk/jfk1110.htm.

After landing in Washington, D.C., Kennedy's body was taken by helicopter to the Naval Medical Center in Bethesda, Maryland. Despite the rough handling, Kennedy's body was still most likely the best available evidence to solve the crime. However, authorities did not bring in the best forensic pathologists in the nation to perform one of the most important autopsies of the century. Instead, it was performed by two military doctors: James J. Humes and J. Thornton Boswell.

Humes and Boswell, administrators at the Naval Medical School, were highly trained doctors, but they were not forensic analysts. This meant that they were not necessarily interested in gathering evidence to be used against a criminal. One author explained, "hospital pathologists such as Humes and Boswell are not trained in the forensic aspect of autopsies or the search for clues in unnatural deaths, nor do they normally preserve evidence for subsequent medical or legal proceedings."[16]

Knowing that they were not experienced in studying gunshot wounds, the doctors called in Dr. Pierre Finck to aid them. Finck was a renowned expert in ballistics and had studied records of gunshots for many years. This qualified Finck as an experienced investigator in cases of a medical-legal nature, involving trauma, violent death, a bullet wound, or an accident. Despite this experience, however, he was still not trained in the forensic aspect of performing an autopsy.

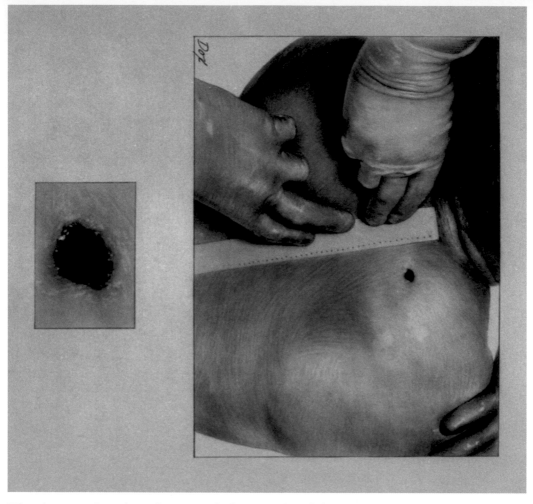

This drawing, based on the original photographs of the JFK autopsy, shows the back wound suffered by Kennedy. His wounds were unquestionably caused by gunshots, and some have questioned whether the doctors who performed the autopsy were qualified to examine that specific type of wound.

A Questionable Autopsy

As the doctors prepared for the autopsy, the room filled with more than 20 observers, including admirals, generals, and agents of the FBI, CIA, and Secret Service. Because witnesses could distract doctors during delicate procedures, it is highly unusual for many people to witness an autopsy. Some reports indicate that all of these spectators tried to tamper with the process of the autopsy. However, the House Select Committee on Assassinations (HSCA), which was

Fake Photos?

The photos of President Kennedy's autopsy were withheld from public viewing from 1963 until 1979, when the Assassinations Records Review Board released them to the general public. However, some have argued that the wounds in the photos do not match the descriptions given to the Warren Commission by autopsy doctors. This has led some to believe that there might be two sets of autopsy photos—and one set is a forgery. This belief is based on forensic science.

When a person is shot, the bullet makes a small hole upon entry and leaves a large exit wound as it continues through the body. Doctors in Dallas stated that Kennedy had a small entrance wound on the side of his skull and a large exit wound in the back of his head, which suggested that the fatal shot came from in front. However, the autopsy photos revealed only a small, neat entrance wound at the back of the president's head. Some researchers have asserted that the publicly released pictures are not of Kennedy:

FBI agents who saw the autopsy images of JFK's skull wound testified under oath … that JFK's fatal skull wound looked nothing at all like the photographs that showed the backside of JFK's skull and scalp intact … Instead, they claimed a sizable rearward skull [hole] was present … that was corroborated by numerous witnesses … including neurosurgeons and pathologists. John Stringer, the autopsy photographer of record, denied that he had taken the photographs of JFK's brain that survive in the [documents].[1]

1. James H. Fetzer, *Murder in Dealey Plaza: What We Know Now that We Didn't Know Then about the Death of JFK.* Chicago, IL: Catfeet Press, 2000, p. 189.

created in 1976 to reinvestigate the murder of JFK, concluded that the onlookers did not significantly hamper the autopsy.

These findings have not convinced many conspiracy theorists, however, who still argue that the autopsy was poorly handled. Many people still claim that no doctor should have allowed the autopsy to be performed as it was. Some medical experts, such as coroner and Warren Commission critic Cyril Wecht, have argued that Kennedy's autopsy was

extremely … sloppy, inept, incomplete, incompetent in many respects, not only on the part of the [doctors] who did this horribly inadequate medical-legal autopsy but on the part of many other people. This is the kind of examination that would not be tolerated in a routine murder case by a good crew of homicide detectives in most major cities of America on ... just a plain ordinary citizen, let alone a [murdered] President.[17]

Nevertheless, both the Warren Commission and the HSCA have confirmed the original autopsy findings. Not only do the reports match each other, they match the reports filed by the surgeons who operated on Kennedy while he was still in Dallas. The handling of his body, however, still remains a questionable component of the JFK murder case for many conspiracy theorists.

Sworn to Secrecy

No one has been able to adequately answer why the autopsy of a murdered president was conducted in such a controversial manner. Some offer a simple explanation: The entire event was out of the ordinary for everyone involved, and there was no legal or medical protocol in place for handling the assassination of the president in the 1960s. After all, the last presidential assassination took

The people who witnessed Kennedy's autopsy were forced to sign agreements that they would not discuss what they witnessed. Some people have argued that this is suspicious, while others point out that it was done to protect the privacy of the victim and his family.

place in 1901. Conspiracy theorists, on the other hand, have formulated dozens of other explanations over the years.

Some believe the high-ranking government officials in the room were hoping to achieve their own goals from the autopsy. For example, the CIA could have wanted the autopsy to show Kennedy was shot by several assassins who could be traced to Cuba, which would allow them to take aggressive actions against Cuban dictator Fidel Castro. The FBI and Secret Service, possibly embarrassed by their failure to protect the president, could have wanted to promote the crazed loner theory, rather than a conspiracy that could have been prevented. Some conspiracy theorists believe that CIA and military officials were actually a part of the assassination.

While the intentions of those in the autopsy room are unknown, it is a matter of record that all military personnel in attendance were sworn to silence under threat of arrest and ordered to sign an official document that read: "You are reminded that you are under verbal orders ... to discuss with no one [the] events connected with your official duties [at the autopsy] ... You are warned that [disobeying] these orders makes you liable to Court Martial proceedings."[18] Court-martial is the term militaries use to describe actions taken in court against military personnel.

For the Kennedys

Conspiracy theorists have made much of the president's unorthodox autopsy, and in 1976, a congressional investigation into the shooting by the HSCA addressed this issue. After interviewing most of the men who were in the autopsy room, the HSCA determined that Robert Kennedy, Jackie Kennedy, and other members of the family were in attendance in Bethesda that evening and refused to leave the premises until the president's body was ready to be moved. This was barely eight hours after the president had been killed, and the Kennedys had only given permission for a partial autopsy, because they wanted to get it over with as soon as possible.

Therefore, during the procedure, Admiral George C. Burkley, White House physician to the president, was acting as an intermediary between the family, the doctors, and others gathered in the room. According to the 1979 HSCA report,

[Dr. Humes] believed there was no question that Dr. Burkley was conveying the wishes of the Kennedy family regarding a full-versus-partial autopsy. Special Agent Sibert [also] told the

Admiral George C. Burkley was the White House physician when Kennedy was president. During JFK's autopsy, Burkley allegedly intervened to protect the privacy of the Kennedy family.

organs and the rest of his body. By 11:00 p.m., doctors had reached the conclusion that one bullet entered the rear of Kennedy's skull and exited the front. Another bullet had entered the president's back at the base of the neck and exited his throat. This wound was widened at Parkland Memorial Hospital by doctors who inserted a tube into it to help Kennedy breathe during the last moments of his life. Government doctors used this as the explanation for why the entry wound was wider than the exit wound on his neck.

committee that he, too, had the impression the Kennedy family was somehow transmitting step-by-step clearances to the [doctors performing the autopsy].[19]

Despite the restrictions placed on the doctors, both Boswell and Humes claimed that they performed a thorough autopsy in the areas of the gunshot wounds. A full autopsy would have involved a complete surgical examination of the president's

Because the autopsy was rushed by JFK's family and was only a partial autopsy, several major mistakes were made. The areas where the bullets entered or left Kennedy's body were not dissected to determine the exact angles and directions that the bullets traveled. For example, Humes simply probed Kennedy's back wound with his finger, which not only changed the shape of the wound but was also an inexact examination to determine the exact nature of the shot.

A Negligent Commission

Further problems were created because of the way X-rays and photographs of the autopsy were handled by officials. The official photographs would have provided an inarguable record of the autopsy. However, most of the official photographs were immediately seized by the government and made confidential. Figuring out why the photos were classified is a guessing game. Some say it was, like the autopsy itself, uniquely handled out of respect for the Kennedy family's privacy. Some believe, however, that the photos showed evidence that Kennedy was shot from the front and the back, therefore proving the existence of two shooters, and the government did not want this to be revealed.

The Warren Commission did not consider the actual autopsy photographs or X-rays before publishing their report. The Assassination Records Review Board claimed that this decision was made by Warren Commission member Earl Warren, who said the actual records were too graphic to be made public. Some autopsy photos and X-rays were examined by the HSCA in the 1970s and eventually released, but the nature and origin of these pictures is debated. Some claim they were fabricated after the autopsy to cover up a conspiracy.

Instead of using photos to determine the cause of the president's death, the Warren Commission was given drawings of his wounds. These were illustrations in pencil made by an artist, who was also not working from the photographs. A doctor described the wounds, and the artist drew them based on instruction. However, the drawings were not as accurate as photographs. For example, the HSCA determined that Kennedy's back wound was drawn higher than the photos revealed. Some conspiracy theorists have suggested that this means the bullet might not have come from the sixth floor of the Texas School Book Depository but from a different location. Despite the questionable value of the illustrations, the Warren Commission used them to create diagrams of the bullet trajectories, which were the paths the bullets took as they passed through the president's head and body.

Questions of Evidence

Other physical evidence generated by the autopsy was also mishandled, according to critics. Under normal circumstances involving a gunshot wound of this type, the remnants of

Occupation: Medical Examiner

Job Description:
A medical examiner, also called a forensic pathologist, is a specialized doctor who is licensed to practice forensic medicine. They conduct autopsies to examine tissue, organs, body fluids, cells, and DNA in an effort to discover the cause of a disease or death. Medical examiners also evaluate blood tests, assist with rape examinations, and do other medical work to help solve crimes.

Education:
Medical examiners must first earn a bachelor's degree, focusing on anatomy and biology. Then, they must graduate from an accredited medical school and complete training in forensic pathology, which takes an additional five or more years after graduating from medical school.

Qualifications:
To find employment, aspiring medical examiners must be certified by the American Board of Pathology to practice forensic pathology, which involves rigorous examination.

Salary:
Annual pay for medical examiners varies widely by region. Salaries range from $100,000 to $250,000.

the brain would have been removed and analyzed to trace the trajectory and direction of the bullet. In addition, pathologists would look for bullet fragments stuck in the brain. Using advanced forensic techniques, they could match the bullet fragments to a specific type of gun—such as the Mannlicher-Carcano that Oswald was accused of using in the assassination.

Humes, Boswell, and Finck conducted a partial autopsy of the brain, but the examination was never fully completed. Many investigators have argued that the incomplete brain

By the Numbers

61

percent of Americans in 2013 who did not believe Oswald acted alone

evidence, the partial autopsy, and the Warren Commission's use of illustrations cast doubt about Oswald's guilt. Moreover, the HSCA also concluded that some aspects of the case were clearly mishandled.

The motives of the government officials involved in the autopsy and the Warren Commission are a matter of speculation. Whatever their intentions, however, they did not take care in performing their duties, and this sloppiness has fueled uncertainty and rumors for decades. One observer stated in 1964, "There has never been a more … conspiratorial, unpatriotic, or endangering course for the United States and the world than the attempt by the United States to hide the truth behind the murder of its recent president."[20]

Chapter Three
Going Ballistic

Investigating any crime—particularly a homicide—is an extremely complicated task. This was especially true in 1963; though forensic science was an established field for investigators to use, its guidelines were not as strictly followed as they are in modern times. For nearly every gun-related murder in the 21st century, police start by examining the crime scene. They collect empty cartridges and bullet fragments, and they examine bullet holes. They trace the trajectories of bullets and find out where the shooter was standing in relation to the victim. This is in addition to standard crime scene investigative procedures, such as looking for fingerprints and other clues related to the suspect.

In crime laboratories, forensic examiners help analyze some of this information. They look for microscopic details on bullets and bullet fragments, which can help police find what type of gun was used in the homicide.

They can perform DNA and fingerprint analysis to narrow down the list of suspects. Medical examiners perform an autopsy on the victim, carefully recording everything they find out, and they prepare a report that includes a section on the ballistics of the gunshot wound.

In forensic science, ballistics refers to the study of evidence related to firearms and bullets. Analysts look at the angle of a bullet's entry into a human body, examine entry and exit wounds, and calculate distances and possible shooter locations. In addition, forensic experts examine firearms and bullet casings to collect fingerprints or any DNA evidence. All these steps help investigators understand how the crime was committed and who their prime suspects are. In the investigation of the assassination of President Kennedy in 1963, however, many of these steps were either skipped, left incomplete, or performed controversially.

Ballistic Analysis

When President John F. Kennedy was assassinated in Dallas, the DPD and FBI agents conducted the forensic ballistics work. Their task was to establish how many bullets were fired, their direction of travel, and their angle of entry. This would allow the authorities to determine if the president was shot from above, behind, the front, or the side. It would also allow them to determine the number of shooters and where they were located when they fired.

The official version of the forensic ballistics findings in the Kennedy case is contained in the Warren report. The Warren Commission concluded Lee Harvey Oswald fired three shots at the president from the sixth-floor

Because President Kennedy was killed by a gunshot, forensic ballistic analysts were some of the most important investigators in the case.

window of the Texas School Book Depository. The commission based its conclusion about the number of shots fired partially on the gun and the three spent shell casings found near the window on the sixth floor of the building. As an added precaution, the Warren Commission ordered tests on the gun to confirm whether it was accurate enough and could be fired quickly enough to be the murder weapon. The forensic ballistic evidence used by the Warren Commission to reconstruct the murder of the president has long been a subject of intense debate.

Critics have questioned the number of shots fired, their trajectories, the gun used, the condition of the bullets that supposedly caused the wounds, Oswald's ability as a marksman, and his palm print on the gun. As with the Kennedy autopsy, there are enough mysteries, riddles, suspicions, and inexplicable actions on the part of government officials to cast doubt on many aspects of the official story.

Murder Weapon?

In any gun-related murder, the firearm allegedly used to commit the crime is one of the most important parts of the investigation. In the investigation

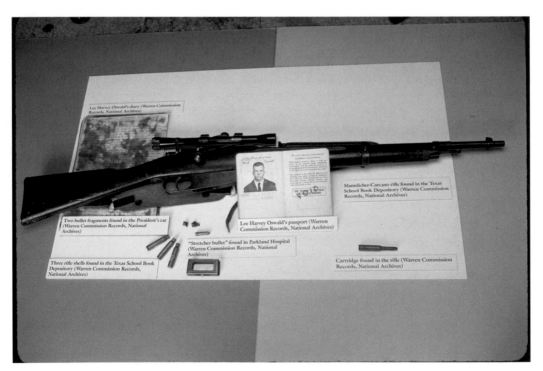

This display shows both Oswald's gun and the used cartridges that he allegedly fired at Kennedy. The gun used a large and lethal caliber of ammunition.

of the Kennedy assassination, even this most basic piece of evidence—the smoking gun that would prove who committed the murder—has been a subject of controversy.

The Warren report stated that the murder weapon was an Italian-made, World War II–era Mannlicher-Carcano. It was chambered to shoot 6.5 mm ammunition, and it was found with a Japanese-made scope attached to it. However, when police first found a gun at the Texas School Book Depository shortly after the president was shot, several law enforcement professionals identified the rifle

as a high-powered, German-made 7.65 mm Mauser. Whatever the make of the rifle, all reports indicate that it had one round in the chamber and that three spent shells were found nearby.

Over the next 24 hours, the DPD reported that the murder weapon was a Mauser, and this was announced on various television and radio news reports. The weapon was also described as a Mauser in a several official DPD reports and sworn statements by the first officers who had seen it. Not long after the assassination, Dallas police stated that the rifle

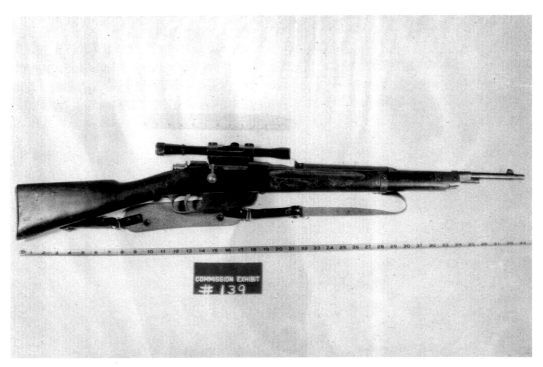

This is the gun that allegedly shot the fatal bullet at Kennedy. Oswald purchased this gun via mail order and paid just $21.45 for both the gun and its scope.

was actually a Mannlicher-Carcano 6.5 mm carbine, serial number C2766.

The misidentification was later explained by experts, who noted the Mauser and the Mannlicher-Carcano look alike. The inconsistency has caused conspiracy theorists to suspect foul play. Though the Warren report definitively identifies the murder weapon as the Mannlicher-Carcano, many have questioned that conclusion. They say the gun make switched after investigators discovered Oswald owned a Mannlicher-Carcano, not a Mauser, so they could frame Oswald for the murder.

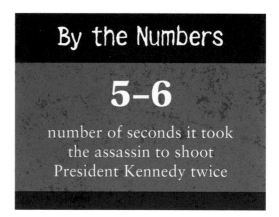

By the Numbers

5–6

number of seconds it took the assassin to shoot President Kennedy twice

A Man and a Gun

The FBI announced that the Mannlicher-Carcano was traced to Klein's Sporting Goods, a mail-order business in Chicago, Illinois. The rifle and scope had been purchased on March 20, 1963, with a money order signed by A. Hidell, whose postal address was PO Box 2915, Dallas, Texas. Oswald was known to use Alek J. Hidell as a fake name, and the handwriting on the money order was analyzed by handwriting experts who matched it to Oswald.

Whether or not Oswald actually handled the Mannlicher-Carcano is another matter of debate. The wooden stock of the gun is rough and does not hold fingerprints well, but Dallas police officer J.C. Day claimed he lifted a partial palm print off a metal part of the rifle the evening of the assassination. However, some argue that the quality of the print is questionable, which means it is possible that it would not have held up if Oswald was taken to court.

There are also rumors that the partial print was put on the rifle after Oswald's death. Those who question the palm print evidence point to conflicting reports regarding when the palm print was supposedly discovered, when it was lifted from the gun, and when it was reported. This claim is also supported by funeral director Paul Groody, who said he was preparing Oswald's body for burial when government agents arrived at the morgue. The agents told Groody they were there to make an examination of Oswald's body.

The agents ordered the mortician to leave the room while they

Tracing It Back

There are many strange aspects concerning the Mannlicher-Carcano rifle traced to Oswald in the Kennedy assassination. This includes the way the weapon—the single most important piece of evidence in the Kennedy case—was handled by law enforcement officials.

The rifle found on the sixth floor of the Texas School Book Depository after the killing was taken to a crime lab by J.C. Day of the crime scene search division of the Dallas Police Department. Day photographed the weapon and said he identified a partial palm print on the gun's barrel. This print was inconclusive, but investigators traced it to Oswald nonetheless. Day did not follow standard procedures, however, as he photographed the palm print before lifting it from the gun. Further investigation was cut short because Day was ordered to give the rifle to an FBI agent named Vince Drain. The agent was never told of the palm print.

Agent Drain took the rifle to Washington, D.C., and gave it to Agent Robert Frazier who, for reasons unknown, kept it in his laboratory for three days. The rifle was then sent back to Dallas. Eventually, the rifle was turned over to an FBI fingerprint expert in Washington, D.C., who could not find any prints on the weapon. The manner in which the rifle was handled, both in Dallas and Washington, hampered the search for usable evidence. Since it was passed from person to person and not kept in a controlled environment, legal experts question whether or not the rifle could be traced to Oswald if he ever made it to a court of law.

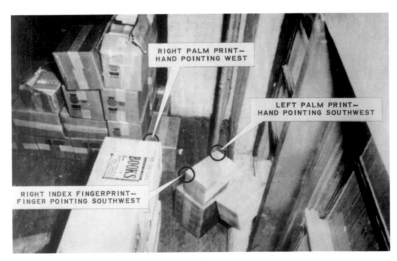

RIGHT PALM PRINT—
HAND POINTING WEST

LEFT PALM PRINT—
HAND POINTING SOUTHWEST

RIGHT INDEX FINGERPRINT—
FINGER POINTING SOUTHWEST

Finding someone's prints at a crime scene is a good way of tying that person to a crime. This photograph explains the fingerprinting done at the Texas School Book Depository Building after the assassination.

worked. After the agents left, Groody found ink on Oswald's palm, which he needed to clean off. He claimed that the only reason they would have inked Oswald's hands was to take finger and palm prints from his body. This seems strange to conspiracy theorists, since finger and palm prints had already been taken at the police station the day Oswald was arrested. The agents said that they simply needed to get some better prints for the record. Conspiracy theorists argue that while agents claimed they were taking additional prints from Oswald, they had actually pushed the Mannlicher-Carcano rifle into Oswald's hand to leave a palm print on it, which would allow them to frame Oswald.

By the Numbers

$21.45

amount Oswald paid for the alleged murder weapon

Who Fired?

In addition to questions surrounding the alleged murder weapon, some believe Oswald never even pulled the trigger. When an individual fires a gun, in addition to leaving fingerprints, they will also have traces of gunpowder on their face, fingers, or clothing. In the 1960s, law enforcement commonly used an analysis called a paraffin test. In this test, warm wax (also called paraffin) is poured over a suspect's skin. The paraffin opens up the pores in the skin while it absorbs chemicals, such as nitrates, that would be left from gunpowder. After the paraffin hardens, it is treated with a chemical that turns nitrates blue. If the wax is spotted with blue dots, it can be used as evidence in court that the suspect shot a firearm.

When Oswald was held for questioning after the assassination, he was given a paraffin test by W.E. Barnes of the Dallas Police Department. The wax was applied to Oswald's hands and his right cheek. His hands showed traces of gunpowder, but his cheek did not. This suggested that he may not have been able to shoot the rifle properly to kill the president. One historian explained, "A positive response on both hands and a negative response on the face is consistent with innocence. It is also consistent with Oswald's claim that he had not fired a rifle on November 22."[21]

Despite the negative results from Oswald's cheek, Dallas police chief Jesse Curry told reporters that the paraffin test was positive and proved Oswald shot the rifle. This information was repeated by law enforcement officers and reported in the *New York Times* and other major media outlets. However, at the time, the FBI's own experiments showed paraffin tests to be unreliable. They could produce both false positives (showing that a person fired a gun even when they did not) and false negatives (showing that a person did not fire a gun even when they did). This meant that the paraffin tests given to Oswald were inconclusive.

Moreover, in November 2005, a study by *New Scientist* magazine determined that gunpowder residue can remain in a room up to eight hours after a gun is fired and can also be picked up by suspects from sources other than firing a gun. Conspiracy theorists have used this to support an argument that Oswald did not fire a gun on the day of the assassination.

Rifle Questions

In addition to the controversial evidence linking the rifle to Oswald, there is also uncertainty about the accuracy of the Mannlicher-Carcano. Some have wondered if the rifle, which cost only $21.45 and was poorly made, could have been used to assassinate someone from a long distance. A 1964 article in *Mechanix Illustrated* stated the opinion that the Mannlicher-Carcano "is crudely made, poorly designed, dangerous and inaccurate ... unreliable on repeat shots, [and] has safety design fault."[22]

The Warren Commission conducted several tests to determine if the Mannlicher-Carcano could have hit its mark from the Texas School Book Depository window. According to the Warren report, the tests showed that the gun was accurate and reliable enough to have been the murder weapon.

In one such test, several FBI agents who were experts in ballistics took the rifle to a firing range to prove its capabilities. The agents took a series of shots at stationary targets 45 feet (14 m), 75 feet (23 m), and 300 feet (91 m) away. Most of the shots hit the target, but the bullets consistently landed slightly high and to the right. With training and experience using the rifle, however, one of the agents testified, "It is a very accurate weapon. The targets we [shot] show that."[23] Regardless, conspiracy theorists claim that it is unlikely Oswald could have killed the president from his position in the sniper's nest, which was 60 feet (18 m) above the street. In addition, they note, Oswald was allegedly shooting at a moving target that was several hundred feet away.

Beyond the rifle's accuracy, conspiracy theorists question whether it could actually fire three rounds in the roughly six-second time frame for the shooting. Those who raise this question typically rely on a minimum estimate of 5.6 seconds for 3 shots to be fired at the presidential motorcade. They say that when one tester, Agent Frazier, tried to shoot the Mannlicher-Carcano 3 times in 5.6 seconds without aiming, he was unable to do so. They point out that the Mannlicher-Carcano is a bolt-action rifle, which means that after each shot, a mechanism has to be pulled back to eject the empty cartridge and then pushed forward to place a fresh round into the chamber of the gun. This not only takes a relatively long time to do, but the rifle would also have to be aimed again and fired. Conspiracy theorists say Frazier could not perform this task for each bullet in less than 2.3 seconds, meaning it took this expert marksman nearly 7 seconds to fire 3 rounds with accuracy.

In March 1964, the Warren Commission ordered the Mannlicher-Carcano rifle retested by sharpshooters at the Infantry Weapons Evaluation Branch of the Ballistics Research Laboratory to determine if Oswald could have fired three rounds in the time they estimated for the shooting. The Warren Commission investigators

theorized it took 5.6 seconds to fire the 2 shots that hit the president, but they claimed all 3 shots (including the first one that missed) may have taken up to 8 seconds. This explanation would make up for the time gap. The National Rifle Association rated all the testers as master marksmen and all were shooters who conducted weapons tests for the military on a daily basis. In contrast, though Oswald had been a Marine, he claimed to have barely touched a weapon since being discharged.

In testing the weapon, the experts fired the Mannlicher-Carcano from a tower, aiming at three stationary targets. They were placed at distances of 175 feet (53 m), 240 feet (73 m), and 265 feet (81 m). The men fired two series of three shots each, a total of eighteen rounds. One marksman was able to make his shots in less than 5.6 seconds; the others required between 6.45 and 8.25 seconds. None of the shooters had any experience with this specific rifle. Based on this test, the Warren Commission believed that the rifle could have fired three rounds in the several seconds it took for the president to be assassinated.

Despite the Warren report's confidence that Oswald could have easily shot three times in roughly eight seconds, conspiracy theorists have raised some issues with their testing. They argue that the test did not account for the fact that Kennedy was in a moving car, that a large tree blocked the motorcade before it came into sight, and that the testers were all expert marksmen. Moreover, some have pointed out that even with the controlled testing environment, none of the marksmen hit the head area of their target, but the Warren report claims that Oswald did so twice. In general, critics of the Warren Commission have said that the tests on the rifle were not accurate or fair representations of what Oswald would have had to do if he were the assassin.

Though the Warren report and many expert investigators have concluded that the Mannlicher-Carcano rifle would have been easily capable of firing three accurate shots in roughly eight seconds, many conspiracy theorists disagree. Based on their interpretation of the test data, it is not possible for even the best shooter to accomplish that task—let alone Oswald, who they claim was not a great marksman. Many theorists also argue that the government has tried to emphasize the fact that they can link the Mannlicher-Carcano to Oswald, even though there is no definitive proof it fired the fatal shots.

A Magic Bullet

Since one shot, typically assumed to be the first shot, missed the limousine's occupants, and the Warren Commission asserted that only three shots were fired, they had to explain how only two bullets caused six wounds to Kennedy and Connally. Arlen Specter, an assistant counselor to the Warren Commission who would later be elected a U.S. Senator, provided the answer.

Specter is credited with authoring the single-bullet theory, which argues that one bullet caused the series of nonfatal wounds, and another bullet actually killed Kennedy. Critics, mainly conspiracy theorists, have mockingly called it the "magic bullet" theory. This magic bullet was allegedly the second shot fired during the assassination, after the first missed. The Warren report stated that this second bullet, known as Commission Exhibit 399, or CE 399, caused six separate, nonfatal wounds in both Kennedy and Connally.

The Warren report described the route of the bullet through the two men: CE 399 entered Kennedy's back and exited through his neck. As Kennedy clutched his throat, the bullet entered Connally at the right side of his back, just below the right armpit. It traveled through his chest in a downward direction and exited below his right pectoral muscle. The bullet continued on, passing through Connally's right wrist, which was resting on his lap, and then buried

Arlen Specter, shown here, is widely credited with coming up with the explanation of how a single bullet could have caused so much damage to both Kennedy and Connally.

itself in his left thigh.

The single-bullet theory is controversial for several reasons. Many find it hard to believe that a single bullet traveled through multiple layers of Kennedy's clothing, skin, and human tissue. After passing through Kennedy's neck, the commission says it passed through the president's necktie knot and entered part of one of Connally's ribs before passing through the front of Connally's chest and shattering the radius bone in his wrist, finally coming to a stop in his thigh.

According to the Warren report, the bullet that did this damage was recovered from the stretcher used to wheel Connally into the operating room when he was taken to Parkland Memorial Hospital. After the governor was placed on an operating table, the stretcher was supposedly wheeled into an elevator and traveled to the ground floor unattended. It was then removed from the elevator by senior hospital engineer Darrell C. Tomlinson, who wheeled

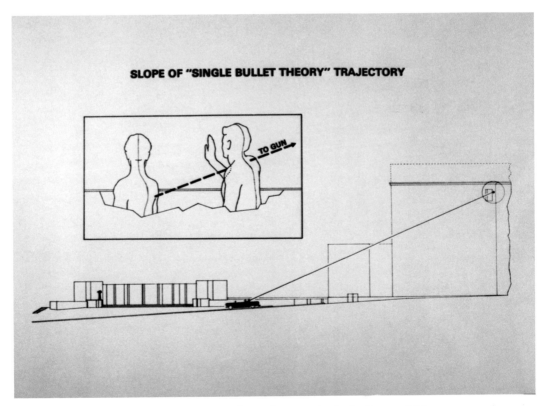

SLOPE OF "SINGLE BULLET THEORY" TRAJECTORY

TO GUN

This illustration, used by the HSCA, shows how a single bullet could have passed through Kennedy and caused a series of wounds to Connally.

Ballistic Uncertainty

James J. Humes was one of the pathologists who conducted President Kennedy's autopsy. Humes was also called before the Warren Commission to comment on the so-called magic bullet theory that supposedly explained the wounds to Kennedy and Connally. The following testimony, in which assistant counsel Arlen Specter questions Humes about the bullet, CE 399, is from the Warren report:

> *Mr. SPECTER. And could [CE 399] have made the wound on Governor Connally's right wrist?*
>
> *Commander HUMES. I think that that is most unlikely … The reason I believe it most unlikely that this [bullet] could have inflicted either of these wounds is that this missile is basically intact; its jacket appears to me to be intact, and I do not understand how it could possibly have left fragments in either of these locations …*
>
> *Mr. SPECTER. Dr. Humes, under your opinion which you have just given us, what effect, if any, would that have on whether this bullet, 399, could have been the one to lodge in Governor Connally's thigh?*
>
> *Commander HUMES. I think that extremely unlikely. The reports [from Parkland Hospital] tell of an entrance wound on the lower midthigh of the Governor, and X-rays taken there are described as showing metallic fragments in the bone, which apparently by this report were not removed and are still present in Governor Connally's thigh. I can't conceive of [how] they came from this [bullet].*[1]

1. Quoted in Investigation of the Assassination of President John F. Kennedy, "Hearings Before the President's Commission on the Assassination of President Kennedy." Washington, DC: United States Government Printing Service, 1964, p. 374–376.

it into the hallway and pushed it up against another stretcher. At that time, the bullet rolled onto the floor and was discovered by Tomlinson, who handed it over to Secret Service agents who were protecting Kennedy's operating room.

There are a number of controversies surrounding the discovery of this bullet. Some say that, rather than coming from the stretcher, the bullet came from the operating room itself. Though Tomlinson's testimony before the Warren Commission was conclusive, because he insisted the bullet fell from a stretcher, some theorists have argued that he is unreliable. If the bullet was actually found in Kennedy's operating room, that would mean that CE 399 fell out of the wound in the president's back and could not have been the bullet that wounded Connally. If that is true, then four or more shots must have been fired that day. Many conspiracy theorists argue that the first shot missed, two hit Kennedy, and at least one hit the governor.

By the Numbers

6

number of wounds allegedly caused by a single bullet fired from Oswald's gun

The Shape of the Bullet

Those who believe in the theory that there were more than three shots point to the physical condition of the magic bullet. As seen in the Warren report, CE 399 was in visibly perfect condition. It was not highly compacted or damaged, as might be expected if it passed through two men. According to the testimony of ballistic experts who appeared before

the Warren Commission, any bullet that passed through the bone and tissue of two people would be flattened, distorted, and broken apart. As Irving Shaw, a former army surgeon who had treated hundreds of gunshot wounds, told Specter, "I feel that there would be some difficulty in explaining all of the wounds as being inflicted by bullet Exhibit 399 without causing more ... deformation of the bullet."[24]

Although many conspiracy theories were built on the condition of the magic bullet, some experts have since contradicted Shaw's testimony. From 1976 to 1977, the HSCA addressed the issue of the undamaged bullet. They noted that the bullet is steel jacketed, which means that the soft lead bullet is plated with a thin layer of steel to travel at a higher velocity. Therefore, since it was protected by a steel jacket, CE 399 could have caused the wounds without becoming distorted or broken. As the HSCA report states, the bullet is a "long, stable, fully jacketed bullet, typical of ammunition often used by the military. Such ammunition tends to pass through body tissue more easily than [other] bullets."[25] Although there was no blood, human tissue, or clothing fibers on the bullet, supporters of the Warren Commission agree that the steel jacket allowed the bullet to penetrate both men and still retain its shape.

Nothing Definitive

Regardless of the physical condition of the bullet, critics claim that a single projectile simply could not have inflicted the wounds doctors observed in the two men. The bullet, they argue, would have had to change course several times and move in a manner that defies physics and logic. To create these wounds, critics say, CE 399 would have had to exit Kennedy's neck, stop in midair, turn to the right, move over, stop again, and then continue on its way through Connally's back. After exiting Connally's body, CE 399 would have had to move downward, go through the right wrist and somehow move over again from his right wrist and into his left thigh.

Supporters of the single-bullet theory point out, however, that Connally was not sitting directly in front of Kennedy, nor was he at the same height. Connally was sitting in a seat that was lower and to the president's left, and he was also turned at an angle so he could wave to people in the crowd. The Warren Commission recreated the scene with models in a similar limousine, and in 1988, the PBS show *Nova* used computer animation to test the theory. Based on photographs from that day, these reconstructions of the crime had Kennedy leaning forward when he was first shot. This would have clearly allowed a bullet to enter his back, exit his lower neck, and hit Connally. However, no photos show Kennedy sitting at this angle, so debate continues over the exact positions of the two men, the physics of the bullet, the effects of bone and clothing on its trajectory, and the blurry photographic evidence used as a basis for the tests.

The Warren report itself uses language that adds doubt to the single-bullet theory. Though the Commission was certain that the single-bullet theory was correct, it could not fully commit to that argument. Describing the single-bullet conclusion, the report read: "the [alignment] of the points of entry was only [suggestive] and not conclusive that one bullet hit both men. The exact positions of the men could not be re-created; thus, the angle could only be approximated."[26]

Missing Shots

The magic bullet is far from the only shot creating controversy. The Warren Commission said that one shot missed the limousine completely and hit the south curb of Main Street, wounding bystander James Tague slightly in the cheek. Immediately after the assassination, a Deputy Sheriff named

Eyewitnesses

There were hundreds of witnesses to Kennedy's assassination in Dealey Plaza on November 22, 1963. However, the Warren Commission did not include most of the eyewitness testimony in their final report. Because of this, some researchers have used those statements to support their argument that there was a conspiracy. Most of the time, theorists point out that around 40 people claimed that there was gunfire coming from a different direction—from the front of the motorcade instead of the back—which would indicate that either Oswald was innocent or there was a second shooter.

Some of the most famous witness testimonies regard the grassy knoll in Dealey Plaza. Because it was a somewhat raised vantage point and had a fence and several trees, some investigators think it would have been the perfect place for another shooter to stand. They support this claim by citing the dozens of eyewitnesses who claim that they saw a figure standing there—some people even claim that they saw someone with a gun pointed right at Kennedy.

Most of the time, however, eyewitness testimony is considered unreliable and easy to fake. Because of the chaos, panic, and confusion surrounding the assassination, the Warren Commission could not sort out which witnesses were telling the truth and which were making up stories. Eyewitnesses frequently fabricate details, and they can be influenced by media outlets or hearing other witnesses. Nevertheless, many theorists argue that the Warren report is incomplete because it excludes a majority of eyewitness statements.

Buddy R. Walthers examined the ground nearby for bullets. Conspiracy theorists insist that Walthers found a bullet lying in the grass, handed it to a man he believed to be an FBI agent, and after that, the bullet was never seen again. However, Walthers himself insists that he never made any statement about finding a bullet, but instead he and the supposed agent could not find anything significant. These conflicting stories add more doubt.

Moreover, the curb was exposed to the elements for nine months before the city dug it up and sent it to the FBI so the bullet mark in the cement could be matched to the same type of bullet used by the Mannlicher-Carcano. FBI analysis was reportedly consistent with the official story—Oswald's first shot missed—but conspiracy theorists and some ballistics experts are still unsure about the flight path of the curb shot.

Allegedly, at least two more gunshot marks were found not far from the murder scene. These bullet marks also have a curious history. According to conspiracy researchers, a bullet mark on a manhole cover in Dealey Plaza lines up perfectly with the Dallas Records Building on Houston Street, where another assassin might have been shooting. Another bullet hit the limousine on the window frame above the rearview mirror. Theorists say this came from almost straight behind the limousine, most likely from the second floor of yet another building. If all these shots were truly fired, then there must have been at least two assassins at work in Dealey Plaza—and maybe more. However, most of the official findings from the Warren Commission, the HSCA, and the reports of independent experts support the three shots, one shooter theory. All the questionable bullet marks are explainable through an analysis of the trajectory of Oswald's first, missed shot.

Chapter Four
Got It on Tape

One of the main reasons the Kennedy assassination is so open to interpretation is because there is no conclusive video evidence of the event. This is largely due to 1963's relatively primitive technology. In modern times, there are thousands of people who watch presidential motorcades while filming with their cell phones or high-end cameras. If an assassination attempt occurred, hundreds of people would have photographic evidence of the event, showing every angle. In the 1960s, however, cell phones did not exist. Even news companies mostly relied on field reporters calling the station from a payphone to deliver the current news to the television station. Moreover, because the president's visit to Dallas was not groundbreaking news, stations were not broadcasting it live.

The largest presence of reporters was actually in a car that was fifth in line behind the presidential limousine in the motorcade. A number of White House reporters were following the president so that they could cover any stories from his trip. Mostly, they were waiting for his speech at the Dallas Trade Mart. Even these journalists, however, were not equipped with cameras. No one expected that tragic world history was going to be written during that drive. Their primary task was to send back snippets of information to news companies they worked for. There was so little interest in the drive, in fact, that the press car was 200 yards (183 m) behind the president's limousine. Throughout the rest of the crowd, there were few recording devices to be found.

This was especially true of the civilian onlookers. Few people had portable cameras, and even fewer had cameras that could record video. People were simply out in Dealey Plaza to see their beloved president ride by on his way to the Trade Mart. Because so few people had any interest in recording the events of the day, little audio or visual evidence

From One Perspective

In 1963, Merriman Smith, a veteran reporter with *United Press International* who was assigned to cover the White House, was on the scene in Dallas when President Kennedy was assassinated. He was riding in the presidential press car, and although it was 200 yards (183 m) behind the president's limousine when the shooting started, his is the only eyewitness report from a professional journalist. His report on the assassination won him a Pulitzer Prize in 1964. He wrote in part,

I was riding in the so-called White House press "pool" car ... Suddenly we heard three loud, almost painfully loud cracks. The first sounded as if it might have been a large firecracker. But the second and third blasts were unmistakable. Gunfire ... One sees history explode before one's eyes and for even the most trained observer, there is a limit to what one can comprehend ... Everybody in our car began shouting at the driver to pull up closer to the president's car. But at this moment, we saw the big [limousine] and a motorcycle escort roar away at high speed.

We screamed at our driver, "Get going, get going." We ... set out down the highway, barely able to keep in sight of the president's car ... They vanished around a curve. When we cleared the same curve we could see where we were heading—Parkland Hospital ... I ran to the side of the [limousine].

The president was face down on the back seat. Mrs. Kennedy made a cradle of her arms around the president's head and bent over him as if she were whispering to him.[1]

1. Merriman Smith, "Eyewitness account of John F. Kennedy assassination," *United Press International*, November 23, 1964. www.upi.com/Eyewitness-account-of-John-F-Kennedy-assassination/51291385108100/.

of the assassination exists. When the Warren Commission set out to investigate the murder, they did uncover one audio recording, one video recording, and a small number of amateur photographs of the events. However, forensic analysts have rarely agreed on how to interpret them. Nearly every expert who examines the film and audio recordings has their own opinion about the events of November 22, 1963.

Sounds of the Scene

One of the most immediate questions about the Kennedy assassination is how many shots were fired that day. If there were more than three, then it is likely there was more than one shooter—and

Merriman Smith (left) had a long history of quality journalism for United Press International. *He was riding in the press car when President Kennedy was assassinated in Dallas.*

the conclusions in the Warren report are wrong. Investigators believed that an audiotape of the assassination would have quickly solved the mystery. After all, gunfire is extremely loud, and even a primitive sound recording device could have picked up on it. Unfortunately, the only sound recording available has not been able to provide a conclusive answer, even after more than 50 years.

During the 1960s, though audio was much easier to capture than video, audio recording devices were still relatively ineffective. Many police departments, including the one in Dallas, recorded radio communications between officers on a machine called a Dictaphone. This machine recorded sounds by interpreting

In the 1960s, recording equipment, shown here on the right, was primitive. Though there is one surviving audio recording from the afternoon of JFK's assassination, it has not been a big help to investigators.

grooves pressed into a thin plastic belt, called a Dictabelt. Purely by chance, there was a Dictabelt recording made around the time Kennedy's motorcade was driving through Dealey Plaza. A motorcycle policeman accidentally left the microphone on his police radio active for about five and a half minutes.

Stressful Sound

Although the Warren Commission did not address the recording, it was thoroughly examined and analyzed by the HSCA in the 1970s. The committee hired James Barger to analyze the tape. Barger was an expert in audio forensics and senior scientist for BBN Technologies, a company that was developing new technologies for acoustic recording and telecommunications in the 1960s.

The tape Barger analyzed did not contain the distinctive sound of rifle shots; instead, it contained mostly static noise mixed with distant voices. To hear the supposed rifle shots, Barger used a sound analysis technique called adaptive filtering. This technique allowed him to subtract the sound of the motorcycle engine, which was the loudest noise on the tape. However, even after applying adaptive filtering techniques, it was still impossible to hear audible shots. Barger was able, however, to identify a series of distinct sound spikes on his computer printout that he believed to be the gunshots.

To investigate further, Barger used a technique called matched filtering, a method to detect barely audible sounds on the Dictabelt. To apply matched filtering, he needed to match the sound waves on the printout to a clear audio record of a rifle firing in Dealey Plaza. This would require a complicated test and required scientists for the HSCA to actually travel to Dallas and record the sound of a rifle shooting in the plaza.

This would give Barger a baseline to work with when applying the matched filter.

Until this test had been done, the HSCA had not been able to confirm—or disprove—the conclusions of the Warren report. With Barger's news, committee members were inspired to figure out the truth. On August 20, 1978, at the direction of the HSCA, the DPD closed Dealey Plaza to the public. Marksmen, using a Mannlicher-Carcano rifle like Oswald's, shot into piles of sandbags in the middle of the street. Barger and a team of audio scientists recorded the shots by using a series of microphones placed along the path of the 1963 motorcade. The scientists then used the audio records to make a series of 2,592 calculations involving 432 combinations of rifle shots and microphone locations. This provided them with a pattern of sound waves called an acoustic fingerprint that could be read like a map and matched to the readings on the Dictabelt recording.

An Answer?

Even after the advanced audio analysis techniques that Barger performed on the Dictaphone recording, there was no clear picture of what truly happened. With the audio technology of the 1960s, especially the unsophisticated Dictabelt that had been preserved for more than

15 years, there was simply not enough clarity to figure out what happened. The microphone picked up engine noise and the sounds of the crowds and was only somewhat able to record the gunfire.

As a result, Barger came to the final conclusion that there was a 50 percent chance that there had only been three shots fired when Kennedy was killed. According to his testimony, it was highly likely that the three shots all came from the direction of the Texas School Book Depository behind the motorcade. The mysterious fourth shot, which most conspiracy theorists insist is real, could not be confirmed by Barger.

The grassy knoll theory is one of the most popular among conspiracy theorists. Not only did a number of eyewitnesses claim that they saw a shooter on or near the grassy knoll, but the expert analysis of the audiotape of the incident was largely inconclusive. Barger confirmed, with 88 percent certainty, that shots had come from the Texas School Book Depository, but he could not come up with a likely conclusion regarding a potential fourth shot.

As a result of the audio forensics, the HSCA declared in its final report in 1979 that Kennedy was "probably assassinated as a result of conspiracy."[27] The committee agreed with the Warren report that Oswald fired three shots from the Book Depository, but after considering Barger's findings, the HSCA reported that there was a high probability that a second gunman shot at, but missed, Kennedy. Although the committee members could not positively identify the other members of the

G. Robert Blakey was an influential member of the HSCA. He supported an alternative theory of Kennedy's assassination, blaming the Italian Mafia for his murder; this assertion has been widely disproven.

conspiracy, the chief counsel and staff director of the committee, G. Robert Blakey, said, "I am now firmly of the opinion that the [Italian Mafia] did it."[28]

Because of all the uncertainties still surrounding the case, there was a lot of disagreement over the HSCA conclusions. Law enforcement experts who studied the Mafia concluded that Kennedy's murder did not bear any of the classic signs of a mob hit. The Mafia had a record of never killing public officials, so it was seen as unlikely that they would murder the most visible public official in the world. In addition, despite a few high-profile hits in public places, most professional Mafia gunmen made sure there were no witnesses, let alone a crowd of people watching a major public event such as the presidential motorcade.

Whether or not Blakey's Mafia assertion is true, his conspiracy conclusions were soon called into question because he said, "If the acoustics come out that we made a mistake somewhere, I think that would end [conspiracy theories]."[29] In the years since the HSCA published its report, numerous scientists and examiners have criticized the forensic audio analysis.

More Confusion

As it turned out, a musician and amateur acoustic researcher named Steve Barber came to the conclusion that the acoustics were wrong. After repeatedly listening to a copy of the Dictabelt recording, Barber was able to pick out the voice of a Dallas police officer speaking in the background of the recording. This was significant, because his speech was in the exact place on the recording where the shots allegedly occurred. However, other verified reports state the policeman uttered those words about one minute after Kennedy was shot. This means that the sound spikes, which the HSCA claimed were definitive proof of additional shots, were actually recorded after the assassination was over.

Barber contacted the FBI, Dallas police, and the National Academy of Sciences (NAS) with his evidence. After a lengthy study, the NAS confirmed Barber's conclusions. The Dictaphone audio was captured well after Kennedy was shot. Despite this evidence, conspiracy theorists came to their own conclusions. Some believed the officer's voice had been deliberately added to the recording after the fact to hide the truth. Others claimed that the Dictabelt machine was simply experiencing an error during that exact moment. However, the NAS tested for these possibilities and concluded "reliable acoustic data do not support a conclusion that there was a second gunman."[30]

Caught on Camera

Forensic audio experts investigating the Kennedy assassination arrived at two conclusions that were almost directly contradictory. Neither side—supporters of the official story and conspiracy theorists—could make a strong case based on Dictaphone evidence. Investigators had to turn to the filmed record of the assassination. Despite the apparently clear footage, there are still dozens of conflicting theories about the murder, and there are countless books, movies, and articles trying to explain the film.

The film of the Kennedy assassination was not made by a professional camera operator or a news crew that had video experience. It was shot by Abraham Zapruder, a woman's clothing

manufacturer who was living in Dallas at the time of the murder. Zapruder's office was in the Dal-Tex Building, directly across the street from the Texas

When Abraham Zapruder set out to attend and film the presidential motorcade on November 22, 1963, no one would have guessed that his video camera, shown here, would capture some of the most important footage in American history.

School Book Depository. A vocal supporter of President Kennedy, Zapruder decided to take time off work to watch Kennedy's motorcade pass through Dealey Plaza. Although he was simply planning to observe the event, he made a fateful decision and went home first to get his Bell & Howell Zoomatic 8 mm movie camera so he could film the president as he passed by.

Zapruder was filming as shots rang out and the president was murdered. Incredibly, his grainy, low-quality, color film, which is just 26 seconds long, is the only clear visual record of Kennedy's murder. As *LIFE* magazine described it, "of all the witnesses to the tragedy, the only [truly accurate] one is the 8-mm movie camera of Abraham Zapruder."[31]

Unfortunately for investigators, each frame of 8 mm film is quite small, so any enlargements made from the tiny frames are typically low quality. Moreover, Zapruder's camera did not have capability to record sound. This left investigators wondering if the film could really help them discover exactly how many shots were fired and at what intervals they occurred. Because the camera shot 18.3 frames of film per second (meaning 1 frame was produced for every .055 seconds), the 26 seconds of film yielded nearly 500 frames. Of those, roughly 105 frames capture the president being struck by 2 bullets: 1 striking him in the neck and the

other hitting him directly in the head.

Forensic photographic analysts have been able to use these individual frames as a "clock," because the camera records film at a perfectly steady rate: 1 frame per .055 seconds. By doing this, they can determine the sequence of events by looking at each individual frame. For example, the Warren Commission divided 105 frames by 18.3 frames per second and determined that the full assassination took place in roughly 5 to 6 seconds.

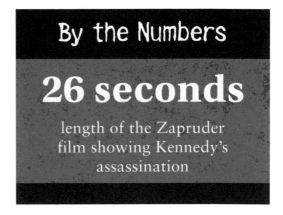

By the Numbers

26 seconds

length of the Zapruder film showing Kennedy's assassination

Zapruder Controversies

Although the Zapruder film provides some important information, it unfortunately does not tell the complete story of the assassination. For example, Kennedy's limousine passes behind a freeway sign at frame 210 and emerges at frame 225. At this time, Kennedy is already grabbing his throat with both hands, his reaction to being shot. This

Problems Filming

With so many questions concerning the Kennedy assassination, even a photographic record is not enough to silence the critics of the Warren report or the HSCA. Many of these doubts come from the unusual and suspicious events surrounding the Zapruder film, which is the clearest known record of the murder.

After the assassination, Abraham Zapruder had at least three copies made of the film. He gave one print to the FBI office in Dallas and one to Secret Service agents who flew it to Washington, D.C., to be analyzed by the National Photographic Interpretation Center, where many copies were made and given to the CIA and other agencies. Zapruder sold the original film reel to *LIFE* magazine, reportedly for more than $150,000. Although a number of individual frames of the film were published in the magazine, the editors did not print frames 313 to 320. These highly graphic frames show the president's head violently moving backward after the fatal shot to his head.

LIFE bought the rights to the film and kept it out of the public eye for 12 years. Americans never got to see the actual movie of Kennedy's murder until 1975. When photographic expert Robert J. Groden finally analyzed the film, he saw what appears to be a shot to the president's head from the front, which would have cast serious doubt on the conclusions of the Warren report and seemingly confirmed a number of different conspiracy theories about multiple shooters.

left the Warren Commission to conclude "the President was probably shot through the neck between frames 210 and 225."[32]

If the Warren Commission had stopped there, the matter of when the president was shot might have been settled. However, the commission added uncertainty to its own conclusion when it added that "a victim of a bullet wound may not react immediately and, in some situations ... the victim may not even know where he has been hit, or when."[33] This suggests the possibility that Kennedy may have been reacting to a shot fired before frame 210.

The Warren Commission determined, based on witness testimony and bullet casings found in the Texas School Book Depository, that three shots were fired at the president's limousine that day. As it examined the Zapruder film, the commission looked for the timing of these three shots. Although the Warren report claims that the Zapruder footage confirms their theories, some people viewed the film evidence and came to different conclusions. Conspiracy researchers insist the film shows that as many as six shots were fired that day in Dealey Plaza.

Most of these alternate theories

state that frame 150 of the film shows the president turning to his right and looking at the grassy knoll. At this point, the Warren Commission said Kennedy was reacting to the first shot fired, the one that missed the car. Critics say that Oswald could not have fired when the president's limo was in that location, because an oak tree would have blocked the view if he was in the sniper's nest on the sixth floor of the Book Depository. There is little doubt, however, that the first shot was fired at this time, because it startled Zapruder, causing his hand to involuntarily jerk, which caused some of the film to get blurry at that particular area.

The president continued his wave until the second shot hit him in the throat. Although the Warren Commission reported that Oswald fired the second shot from behind the president, critics say frames 188 through 191 of the Zapruder film seem to show the president's body pushed backward by the force of the bullet. They contend that this proves shot two came from the front, either from the grassy knoll or a different area. This suggests either multiple shooters or Oswald's innocence. At this point, the limousine disappears from view behind a highway sign, but when it emerges at frame 225, the president is clearly reaching for his throat with both hands.

At this point, conspiracy researchers believe more shots are fired. A third shot, they argue, was fired at almost the same time as the second. This missed Kennedy and hit Governor Connally in the chest. This is an alternative explanation to the single-bullet theory, which details how the second shot went through Kennedy to wound Connally. The Zapruder film clearly shows Connally holding his white Stetson cowboy hat in his right hand—but the single-bullet theory claims the second shot shattered his wrist. Some theorists who have studied the film claim that it would have been impossible for the governor to hang onto his hat if he was also shot through the wrist by this bullet, so there simply must have been an additional shot. Others say, however, that it would not be unusual for him to continue gripping his hat as an involuntary reflex.

Theorists also claim the alleged third shot did not come from the sixth-floor

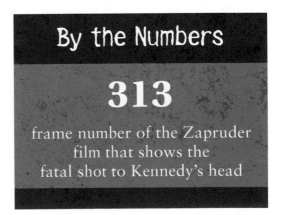

By the Numbers

313

frame number of the Zapruder film that shows the fatal shot to Kennedy's head

sniper nest in the Book Depository, but from the opposite end of the building on a lower floor. Yet another shot, the fourth bullet that conspiracy theorists claim is in the film, is also fired in this time frame, and strikes Kennedy in the middle of his back, slightly below the shoulder. This bullet might have been fired from a second-floor window of the Dal-Tex Building.

The Infamous Grassy Knoll

The shot that killed the president is clearly shown on frame 313, hitting him in the right temple and leaving a large hole in the side of his head. Despite being the obvious cause of Kennedy's death, this shot has also generated its share of controversy. According to common conspiracy theories, this fatal blow was the fifth

The grassy knoll, a prominent feature in Dealey Plaza shown here, has been a central point of debate among conspiracy theorists and those who support the official story of the JFK assassination. Some believe another shooter was located here.

shot fired that day, not the third, as the Warren Commission report asserts. Some researchers also claim that the Zapruder film clearly shows Kennedy's body violently thrown back and to the left as if the shot came from the front right—which would be the grassy knoll, not the Book Depository.

When the HSCA looked into this issue, it was unable to determine whether this proved that Kennedy was shot from the front. Rather, their expert analysis could only show that it was possible he was shot from the back, but it was also possible he was shot from the front. Michael Baden, head of the committee's forensic pathology panel, concluded that

> nerve damage from a bullet entering [the back of] the President's head could have caused his back muscles to tighten which, in turn, could have caused his head to move toward the rear ... the rearward movement of the President's head would not be fundamentally inconsistent with a bullet striking from the rear.[34]

Some people, including many conspiracy theorists, disagree with that conclusion. One conspiracy researcher claimed, "any bullet striking JFK at the base of his skull from Oswald's supposed perch would have created a [large] exit wound in JFK's face ... including a good portion of the right forehead, the entire right eye socket and part of the cheekbone."[35] The president did not have this sort of wound, however, and this issue has never been definitively resolved by either government agencies or conspiracy researchers.

Furthermore, those who believe that there were two shooters also claim that a sixth shot came about a half-second after Kennedy's head wound. Shot six, which allegedly came from the same window in the Book Depository as shot three, hit Connally, shattering his right wrist and exiting into his thigh. The governor reacted to this shot by dropping his hat. If all these shots were fired, as conspiracy theorists say, then there must have been at least two assassins at work in Dealey Plaza—and maybe more. Some theorists also claim that none of the shots seem to have come from Oswald's sniper's nest in the Book Depository.

Secret Assassins?

Some take the theory of two shooters even further and make the shocking claim that Secret Service agents were involved with the plot to kill the president. To support this unproven claim, they point out the inaction of the agents when the shots were raining down on

A Tricky Picture

After Lee Harvey Oswald was taken into custody, Dallas police said they found several suspicious photographs at Oswald's home. The pictures show Oswald posing as a Communist revolutionary, standing in his backyard with a pistol on his right hip, wielding a rifle in his left hand and two pro-Communist newspapers in his right. These photos were leaked to the press by authorities, and one of them appeared on the cover of *LIFE* magazine on February 21, 1964. Some argue that this was done to convince the public that Oswald was guilty.

Oswald was shown these photographs after his arrest, and he claimed a photographic expert faked the image to make him look bad. He said, "That picture is not mine, but the face is mine. The picture has been made by superimposing my face. The other part of the picture is not me at all, and I have never seen this picture before."[1]

After Oswald's death, assassination researchers and photograph experts studied these pictures extensively. Some found issues concerning the shadows in the pictures. For example, there is a dark shadow under Oswald's nose, meaning the sun was directly overhead at around noon when the picture was taken—but Oswald's neck is dark on one side and light on the other, which could indicate that this part of the photo was taken at 10:00 a.m., when the sun was to the side. The shadow of his body extends far out behind Oswald's body, and experts say this is a 4:00 p.m. shadow. Therefore, some have argued, the photos appear to be pasted together from other pictures.

For the most part, however, the photograph of Oswald in his backyard, equipped with several weapons and holding newspapers supporting Communism, appears to be a real picture. Numerous forensic photograph examiners and visual analysts have supported the official story: It is really Oswald.

1. Quoted in Pamela J. Ray, *To Kill a Country*. Bloomington, IN: AuthorHouse, 2009, p. 41.

the motorcade. Richard Belzer, conspiracy theorist and outspoken critic of the Warren Commission wrote,

photos taken at the time of the shooting show a bizarre lack of reaction from the agents riding behind Kennedy. While the president grasps his throat, Secret Service agents are looking around

… With the exception of Clint Hill, an agent brought in at the last minute by the First Lady, they make no move to shield the president from further gunfire.

Most [strange], after the first shot is fired, Kennedy's driver, Secret Service Agent William Greer,

Despite Oswald's claims of forgery, nearly all experts agree that he is actually the one posing in this photo, which was one in a series that showed him holding pro-Communist newspapers and wielding firearms.

actually brings the car to a halt. Though he testified that he kept the [car] moving ... at all times ... the car [slows] to nearly a standstill until the fatal bullet hits its mark.[36]

To investigate these and other claims, Zapruder's film of Kennedy's murder has become one of the most studied pieces of film in history. It was an essential part of the Warren Commission hearings, and video evidence is typically conclusive. However, to confuse matters further, there are some conspiracy theorists who believe that even this one vital piece of photographic evidence has been faked or altered. To support this theory, they follow the chain of possession of the film from Zapruder to the FBI.

After the assassination, Abraham

Zapruder had a small number of copies made of the film. He sold the original to *LIFE* magazine the day after the assassination, and they kept it secret for more than 10 years. Conspiracy theorists, however, suggest that the Secret Service was in possession of the original print of the film for about 18 hours—after it was developed but before it was sold to *LIFE*. They claim that it was altered, with images resized, frames removed, important details erased, and the film manipulated. Some who claim to have seen the original film say that it showed blood and brains coming out of the back of Kennedy's head with the fatal shot, which would indicate a shot from the front. These claims, however, are suspect, because Zapruder only held the original film for one day before selling it to *LIFE*.

Lost Visual Proof?

In addition to the Zapruder film, there are several important photographic records of the assassination that are equally controversial. More mysteriously, there are also people who insist that they captured the assassination on film but also claim that their evidence was destroyed or taken by government agents.

Beverly Oliver, a nightclub singer, claims she was standing on the other side of the street when Kennedy was shot. She has said she filmed the scene with a brand-new movie camera and had a clear view of the grassy knoll. Oliver says she saw Kennedy's head shot and saw a figure and a puff of smoke from the area of the grassy knoll. After the assassination, Oliver claimed the FBI confronted her and took her film, which was never seen. However, most people doubt Oliver's claims. She did not come forward until 1970, and most of her claims about the events surrounding the assassination have been disproved.

Like Oliver, another questionable witness has claimed to have filmed the assassination. A young soldier named Gordon Arnold claimed he was shooting a home movie of the president from the grassy knoll. Arnold, who had just finished basic training exercises in the military, has said he was startled to hear and feel a bullet fly by his head from behind. Arnold has said he quickly dropped to the ground as a reaction before hearing another shot directly over his head. Not long after this, he has said two policemen approached him. Arnold claimed that one of the officers was shaking and crying, holding a shotgun in his hand. He supposedly kicked Arnold and told him to stand up. Arnold has said he immediately handed over his film, which the officer destroyed on the spot. This story has been disputed for a number of reasons. Arnold is not visible in any confirmed photographs taken of the scene, and he has told several different versions of the story. Moreover, he did not come forward with this information until the 1970s.

Real Visual Proof

Mary Ann Moorman, however, was a proven eyewitness in Dealey Plaza when the president was killed. Moorman was standing across the street from the grassy knoll and managed to take a photograph just a fraction of a second before Kennedy was fatally shot in the head. In the years after the assassination, researchers studying the photograph have claimed they can see a man in the back of the picture. This figure has been called the Badge Man because of a shiny object on his chest—possibly a police badge. This figure is hard to make out, but some have argued he appears to be holding a rifle and a puff of smoke can be seen coming out of the barrel. Conspiracy theorists speculate that the Badge Man fired the fatal shot that killed Kennedy and was dressed as a policeman so he could blend into the crowd.

This barely visible figure is open to interpretation. First of all, the original picture is not high quality, even based on the standards of the 1960s. Moreover, the Badge Man is little more than a tiny speck in an indistinct background. During its investigation, the HSCA sent the original image to the Rochester Institute of Technology, a world leader in advanced photographic analysis, and analysts there could not confirm the presence of a human figure in the background of the picture. If it had been taken with a modern-day digital camera, it is possible that it could have been more useful to investigators. As it stands, it is simply a photograph taken just before the assassination of John F. Kennedy. The existence of a Badge Man cannot be proven or disproven.

Regardless of the arguments of many conspiracy theorists, the prime suspect in the assassination is still Lee Harvey Oswald. He was a man with a checkered past, training with and access to firearms, and a motivation to murder President Kennedy. While some have concluded that he did not act alone, it is highly likely that he still fired shots at JFK on November 22, 1963.

Chapter Five
Exploring Oswald

The prime suspect in one of the most notorious crimes of the 20th century was murdered before he had his day in court. Lee Harvey Oswald never had a chance to argue his innocence or defend himself, but some experts believe he may have argued that he was mentally unsound. Because he was never put on trial, he did not undergo a psychological evaluation that would have informed investigators about his state of mind. During the course of the Warren Commission and the HSCA's examination of the case, however, some forensic psychologists have attempted to understand the mind of the alleged murderer.

The job of forensic psychologists is to understand the mental state of suspected criminals. They combine the fields of legal and psychological analysis to determine whether an accused criminal is actually responsible for their crimes. In many countries, even if a person confesses to a serious offense, such as murder, they can still be found not guilty by reason of insanity. In cases such as this, a person is typically confined to a mental hospital, where they can attempt to improve their mental health, instead of a prison cell. If Oswald's trial ever took place, his attorneys may have argued that he was insane.

The Warren Commission, though it was not created as a way of putting Oswald on trial, determined that they were not certain of his mental health at the time he allegedly committed the murder. "Since Oswald is dead," the report read, "the Commission is not able to reach any definite conclusions as to whether or not he was 'sane' [by] legal standards."[37] The report did include an investigation, however, into the potential mental state of Oswald during the years leading up to the murder. In the decades since the assassination, other psychologists have also examined Oswald's case files and tried to figure out what was going on in his head.

Because it is impossible to perform a full psychiatric evaluation without the subject available, no psychologist has been able to fully or accurately diagnose any mental health issues Oswald may have had. The public's perception of him has ranged from thinking he is an attention-seeking loner to an evil Communist sympathizer to a helpless victim set up to take the blame. The only thing conspiracy researchers and government authorities can agree on in this case is the fact that Oswald was emotionally unstable and mentally troubled in the years leading up to 1963.

By the Numbers

20

number of times Lee Harvey Oswald moved in his youth

A Harsh Youth

Lee Harvey Oswald was born in New Orleans on October 18, 1939, two months after his father died suddenly of a heart attack. He was intelligent, and before he started high school, he had a record of average grades and few behavioral problems in school. To his family, he seemed to be a bright child. His mother, Marguerite Oswald, testified before the Warren Commission: "Lee has wisdom without education. From a very small child ... Lee seemed to know the answers to things without schooling. That type of child ... is bored with schooling because he is a little advanced ... Lee read history books, books too deep for a child that age."[38]

When Lee was 6 years old, his mother married Edwin A. Ekdahl, who was nearly 20 years older than her. Lee took to Ekdahl right away, as Oswald's half-brother John Pic told the Warren Commission: "I think Lee found in him the father he never had. He had treated him real good ... Mr. Ekdahl treated all of us like his own children."[39] However, the marriage did not last long, and when Oswald was nine years old, his mother divorced Ekdahl. Although Oswald was asked to testify at the divorce trial, he refused.

After the divorce, Marguerite often left Lee on his own while she was at work, and Lee's older brother, Robert Oswald, lived at an orphanage. Lee got up every morning, got dressed, ate, and went to school alone. After school, he waited in an empty house until his mother returned. Neighbors

As a young man, Lee Harvey Oswald had a difficult life. His single mother struggled to support the family, and he moved around a lot.

Paper Evaluation

When Lee Harvey Oswald was undergoing psychological evaluation at the Youth House in 1953, he was given a test that asked him to draw human figures. Oswald was told to draw several pictures, each featuring an individual of his choice. The results were analyzed by psychiatrist Irving Sokolow, who wrote that Oswald's drawings were "empty, poor characterizations of persons approximately the same age ... They reflect a considerable amount of impoverishment in the social and emotional areas ... [Oswald] appears slightly withdrawn ... He exhibits some difficulty in relationship to [his mother]."[1]

This kind of drawing test was popular in the mid-20th century because subjects could create a wide variety of pictures that psychologists could examine to reveal their mental state. Psychological forensic experts also used the drawings in court as a way to argue for or against someone's mental stability. Today, however, the test is considered unreliable. There are no set standards to evaluate the patient's drawings other than speculation. In Oswald's case, however, it is known through interviews with friends and family that he had had a hard time relating to others, which confirms at least part of Sokolow's diagnosis.

1. Warren Commission, "Commission Exhibit 1339: Youth House Psychologists Examination Report," Kennedy Assassination Home Page. mcadams.posc.mu.edu/sokolow.htm.

testified to the Warren Commission that during this period, Marguerite was aggressive, while Lee was quick to anger and began slacking in school. It was also revealed that the two of them had an unusually close relationship.

Another New City

Though Oswald and his family were never truly in poverty, they did not have a lot of money, and the family moved 20 times before he was 18 years old. He attended more than 10 different schools. They mostly lived in New Orleans and Dallas, but when Oswald was 13, they moved to New York City to stay with John Pic, who had joined the Coast Guard and was stationed there. Oswald was moody and withdrawn, possibly because he felt like he did not fit in at school. Because he was from the South, his manner of dress and speech brought him unwanted attention from bullies, and students often harassed him. Rather than fight back, Oswald cut classes, spending many of his school days at the Bronx Zoo, studying the animals. Oswald was prone to emotional outbursts, and at one point, he threatened to stab Pic's wife with a small pocketknife.

Oswald's truancy problem soon became critical when he missed nearly a month of school without permission. The school recommended that Marguerite take her son to a psychiatrist, but Oswald refused to go, saying he would not visit what he called a "head shrinker or nut doctor."[40] However, in 1953, the school forced Oswald to appear before a judge in juvenile court, and he was ordered to live in a residential facility for psychiatric evaluation. This institution was called the Youth House. There, he was interviewed by psychiatric social worker Evelyn Strickman, who took a special interest in him. She wrote in a report,

> *This is a seriously detached withdrawn youngster who has preserved some ability to relate but is very hard to reach ... What is really surprising is that this boy has not lost entirely his ability to communicate with other people because he has been leading such a detached, solitary existence for most of his life ... [H]e feels almost as if there is a veil between him and other people through which they cannot reach him but he prefers this ... He acknowledges*

> *fantasies about being all powerful and being able to do anything that he wanted. When I asked [if] this ever involved hurting or killing people, he said that it did sometimes.*[41]

Another psychiatrist, Dr. Renatus Hartogs, diagnosed Oswald as having a "personality pattern disturbance with schizoid features and passive aggressive tendencies."[42] A schizoid personality disorder is a mental illness in which a person shows a lack of interest in social relationships and a preference for a solitary lifestyle. Other symptoms include secretiveness and emotional distance. People who exhibit passive-aggressive behavior deal with their problems by acting stubborn, resentful, sullen, or helpless. According to scholars, "individuals with this disturbance are extremely introverted and shy but are prone to intense outbursts of anger and rage ... Furthermore, Dr. Hartogs concluded that Oswald was potentially dangerous to other people and had a [tendency] to act out explosively and aggressively."[43]

It is important to note that, despite these negative diagnoses, Oswald was a troubled teenager when he was evaluated. His alleged assassination of President Kennedy took place 10 years after these psychological assessments, and a lot happened in

An Assassin's Psychology

On the day after President Kennedy was assassinated, a New York reporter called psychiatrist Renatus Hartogs to make a statement on television about why someone might kill the president. Unbeknownst to the reporter, Hartogs was the doctor who had given 13-year-old Lee Harvey Oswald his psychiatric evaluation when he was placed in the Youth House for truancy in 1953. He later testified before the Warren Commission concerning what he had said to the reporter about the mental health of any individual who would assassinate a president:

A person who would commit such an act has been very likely a mentally disturbed person, who has a personal grudge against persons in authority, and very likely is a person who in his search to overcome his own insignificance and helplessness will try to commit an act which will make others frightened, which will shatter the world, which will make other people insecure, as if he wanted to [get rid of] his own insecurity through his own act.[1]

1. Quoted in Gary W. O'Brien, *Oswald's Politics*. Victoria, BC: Trafford, 2010, p. 13.

his life during that time span. Though the Warren report and some others have used his psychiatric history against him, some conspiracy theorists have argued that it is irrelevant to his actions—or his lack thereof—on November 22, 1963.

Turning to Politics

Hartogs recommended that Oswald receive extensive psychiatric treatment, but before this could happen, Marguerite took him back to New Orleans. His grades were still poor when he returned to school, and he dropped out shortly after.

Despite his lack of formal education,

Oswald was a frequent reader who checked out scholarly material from the local library. When he was 15, Oswald read *Das Kapital* and *The Communist Manifesto*, two books written by German intellectual Karl Marx in the mid-19th century. Marx wrote about average workers, called the proletariat, and their struggles with factory and farm owners, called the bourgeoisie. Marx believed that the proletariat should take control of all factories and farms and eliminate the bourgeoisie. Everyone in society would then be equal, and all workers would equally share the profits. Followers of Marx, called Marxists,

Marguerite Oswald, shown here, was forced to move around during her son's youth, and as a result, he was unable to receive the psychiatric treatment he may have needed.

strongly opposed the American capitalist system. In fact, Marxism was the inspiration for the Communism that spread during the 20th century.

By the time Oswald found Marx's books in the library in the 1950s, Marxism was widely despised in the United States. The system was associated with the Communist government of the Soviet Union, which was considered a major threat to the national security of the United States at that time. Suspected Marxists and Communist sympathizers were fired from their jobs, harassed by the FBI, and even jailed for their political beliefs. Despite this, Oswald claimed allegiance to Marxism and the Soviet Union.

A New Identity

Although he was interested in Marxism, Oswald was also eager to join the American military. As Pic put it, "he did it for the same reasons that I did it ... to get from out and under ... [our mother's] oppression."[44] When he was 17, the youngest age possible at the time, he joined up with the United States Marine Corps. The year was 1956.

During his three-year tour of duty in the Marines, Oswald was trained in a variety of different fields. Though he graduated in the bottom 10 of his

Despite his support of Communism, Oswald's dream was to join the United States Marine Corps. He enlisted at the age of 17 and served for 3 years.

class on map reading and air traffic control, he was in the top 10 in his class on radar communication. He was eventually stationed at a naval air base installation in Atsugi, Japan. Because of his success in the course on operating radar, Oswald was given a job as an aircraft director for the naval base.

Even as a member of the armed forces, he could not keep himself from getting into trouble. In 1957, he accidentally shot himself in the arm with a small pistol that he was not supposed to have in his possession. He was charged with a military offense, called a court-martial, and put on probation; unless he kept out of trouble for the next 6 months, he would be sentenced to 20 days of hard labor. This was only the beginning of his problems.

Oswald also took to drinking alcohol while in the Marines and became loud and outgoing when drunk. After a minor scuffle with a fellow Marine, Oswald faced another court-martial and was sentenced to 28 days of hard labor in confinement. After his release, he was bitter and withdrawn, telling a fellow Marine, "I've seen enough of a democratic society ... When I get out I'm going to try something else."[45]

Some have speculated that his two court-martials caused Oswald to resent the Marines and contact Japanese Communist agents, offering to become a spy. Some reports claim that Oswald was seen taking photographs of buildings and radar equipment around the Atsugi base. In addition, other Marines noticed that he had become more aggressive and was spending time with unidentified Japanese people both near the base and in the larger city of Tokyo.

During his entire tour of duty, Oswald was extremely interested in the Soviet Union, and he started studying the Russian language. He was also frequently seen reading newspapers, in both English and Russian, that were pro-Communist and playing Soviet nationalist music around the barracks. He also got into in-depth discussions with his fellow Marines about international affairs. He was particularly interested in the Soviet Union and Cuba, which was becoming a Communist country. Though he never openly admitted to being a Communist, other members of his unit kidded him about being a spy and called him by a Russian nickname: "Oswaldkovich."

A Different Union

When Oswald was asked by a fellow Marine why he did not go out at night like the other men, he said he was saving his money for something important. On October 16, 1959, two weeks after receiving an honorable discharge from the Marines, Oswald used that money to defect to the Soviet Union. There has been some speculation that Soviet spies helped him arrive in Moscow, the U.S.S.R.'s capital, but these suspicions have never been confirmed. It is likely that Oswald simply wanted to give Communism a try.

The Warren report attempts to explain Oswald's motives, saying he was unhappy with the United States and chose to move to the Soviet Union in search of a better life. Conspiracy researchers point out, however, that Oswald had been trying to learn Russian during his career in the Marines. He also had access to confidential information because of his job operating radar; because of these two facts, some theorists believe Oswald had been trained to be a Soviet spy. However, in an interview on the TV program *Frontline*, Robert Oswald said he discussed the move with his brother, who said he wanted to do something bold and dramatic in the style of the American author Ernest Hemingway. Robert Oswald said, "He wants to get some experience and write about it."[46] Hemingway had lived in Cuba, and Oswald wanted to live in the U.S.S.R.

The Russians, however, did not

The United States and the U.S.S.R., whose flag is shown here, were bitter enemies throughout the 20th century. Oswald believed that the Soviet style of Communist government was far superior to the capitalist government of America.

seem to trust Oswald at all. Not long after he arrived in the capital city of Moscow, a Soviet government official refused Oswald's application for citizenship and informed him that he must leave the country immediately. Oswald recorded his feelings and reaction to the news in his diary:

> *I am shocked!! My dreams! I retire to my room. I have $100 left. I have waited for two years to be accepted. My fondest dreams are shattered ... because of bad planning. I planned too much! ... I decide to end it. Soak wrist in cold water to numb the pain. Then slash my left wrist ... Somewhere, a violin plays, as I watch my life whirl away.*[47]

Despite Oswald's description, the cut was not deep, and he was found by someone shortly after his suicide attempt. In the aftermath of his outburst, he was taken to a hospital and given five stitches. The next morning, Oswald was transferred to the psychiatric ward of the hospital, where he was put under close observation for a few days by Soviet psychiatrists. These doctors concluded that he was probably still mentally vulnerable, but he was transferred to the regular wards and allowed to stay in the U.S.S.R. as he recovered.

In early November 1959, a few days after Oswald was released from the hospital, he traveled to the U.S. Embassy in Moscow and dramatically renounced his citizenship, turning in his passport to stunned officials. He met with a senior member of the American delegation to the U.S.S.R., and he demanded that he be allowed to dissolve his citizenship. The official was reluctant to allow Oswald to defect, and he was alarmed when Oswald declared that he had already made an offer to tell Soviet officials confidential information about his time in the Marine Corps.

For the next several months, he spent his days alone, studying Russian in his hotel room. Then, on January 4, 1960, Oswald was given papers that allowed him to remain in the U.S.S.R. as a guest. He was also told he would be transferred to the city of Minsk, where he would go to work in a factory. Despite being allowed to stay, Oswald did not find much happiness in his new surroundings. He quickly realized that the Soviet Union was a tightly regimented society where corrupt officials had total control over average citizens. After being forced to attend mandatory Communist Party meetings every other day, Oswald wrote, "I am starting to reconsider my desire about staying. The work is drab [boring] ... No night clubs or bowling alleys ... I have had enough."[48]

By the Numbers

17

age at which Lee Harvey Oswald joined the Marines

A Marriage

In February 1961, the same young man who had angrily renounced his citizenship at the U.S. Embassy wrote a short, businesslike letter to the same embassy. Oswald requested the return of his passport and expressed the desire to return home, believing he still retained the full rights of an American citizen. They told him that they needed to consider his request, and he needed to return to Moscow to meet in person.

At around the same time, Oswald was dating 19-year-old Marina Nikolayevna Prusakova. The couple had met at a dance hall in Minsk, and Marina was quite impressed with Oswald. She thought he was a Soviet citizen because of the way he acted and because he was fluent in Russian. After going on a number of dates and attending some dances, Oswald asked Marina to marry him. In April 1961, the two were married in the Soviet Union. They soon had a baby together, June Lee Oswald,

who was born on February 15, 1962. Around this same time, Oswald was attempting to find a way to exit the U.S.S.R. with his new family and return to the United States.

Despite the fact that he renounced his American citizenship, and that he had been living in the Soviet Union for a few years, the embassy allowed the couple and their infant to return to the United States in May 1962. Once he arrived back in his home country, Oswald achieved a small degree of notoriety in the press as a Marine who had defected and then returned to the United States.

No Normal Life

The Oswalds settled down in Fort Worth, Texas, a city near Dallas, in June 1962. At first, the couple socialized with the small community of immigrants from Russia and other Eastern European countries in the Dallas-Fort Worth area. Because the family did not have much money, many prominent members of the Russian community wanted to help them. However, Oswald resented their assistance, and the family was eventually rejected because he was outspoken and rude.

Many of his friends and family were also shocked when they learned that Oswald was physically abusing Marina. Just as he had in Russia,

Lee Harvey Oswald met Marina Prusakova shortly before he returned to the United States from the Soviet Union. They were married and had a baby girl, June Lee, before they were able to come to America and settle down in Texas.

Oswald was growing increasingly unhappy with his life in America. In some of his spare time, he struggled to write about his experiences in the Soviet Union. His brother Robert stated, "He wanted to get his manuscript published if anybody was interested. He had an interesting experience and he had a Russian wife. People ought to take note of this, that he should be interesting."[49] He wanted some kind of attention, or for someone to acknowledge his unique life.

Failing to publish his memoir, Oswald began looking for a job, but his aggressive and seemingly random behavior continued. In late March 1963, according to Marina, Oswald asked her to take the famous backyard photographs of him holding his rifle and several Communist newspapers. Marina did not really understand why he wanted these pictures taken, but he claimed that he wanted June to have one when she grew up. When Marina asked him why their young daughter would want a photo of him holding guns, Oswald said, "To remember Papa by sometime."[50] After the assassination of Kennedy, these photographs would become a subject of widespread controversy. Oswald claimed that the government had simply pasted his face onto the body of someone else. His wife, the photographer, testified that she took

the pictures and even wrote on the back of one of them, "Hunter of Fascists Ha. Ha"[51] in Russian.

Another Attempt

Roughly around the same time as these photographs were taken, Oswald was coming up with a plan to assassinate a popular right-wing political leader, retired general Edwin A. Walker, who lived in Dallas. Walker was an outspoken supporter of segregation (keeping black and white Americans separate) and a loud voice against Communism. He was a controversial figure and often gave speeches at meetings of extremely conservative political organizations, such as the John Birch Society. Oswald compared Walker to Germany's Nazi dictator Adolf Hitler.

According to testimony given to the Warren Commission by Marina, Oswald kept Walker's home under surveillance and even took several photos of the back of his house. Oswald spent hours studying maps of Walker's neighborhood and his photos of Walker's house. According to the Warren report, on April 10, 1963, Oswald left home with his Mannlicher-Carcano rifle and traveled to Walker's house. After he had left, Marina discovered the two backyard photos of Oswald, along with a long note, written in Russian. In it, Oswald told Marina that he might not return home and that he paid the

Investigators have concluded that Oswald's first attempt at assassinating a powerful political figure was retired general Edwin Walker. Oswald came close to killing him, but his aim was slightly off, leaving Walker unharmed.

A Convinced Brother

Psychologists, conspiracy theorists, government officials, and average citizens have argued over Lee Harvey Oswald's guilt or innocence for decades. However, the person who arguably knew him best, his brother Robert Oswald, has little doubt that Lee shot and killed President Kennedy and Officer J.D. Tippit. He made this point clear in an interview for the TV program *Frontline*:

> *There is no question in my mind that Lee was responsible for the three shots fired, two of the shots hitting the president and killing him. There is no question in my mind that he also shot Officer Tippit ... You look at the factual data, you look at the rifle, you look at the pistol ownership, you ... look at the general opportunity—he was present. He wasn't present when they took a head count [at the Texas School Book Depository].*
>
> *You look at all the data there, and it comes up to one conclusion as far as I'm concerned—the Warren Commission was correct ... I would love to be able to say that Lee was not involved in any way whatsoever, or much less to the extent that I believe that he was ... But the facts are there ... True, no one saw him actually pull the trigger on the president but ... his presence in the building was there. What he did after he left the building is known: bus ride, taxi ride, [his home], pick up the pistol, leave, shoot the police officer. Five or six eyewitnesses there. You can't set that aside ... I'd love to do that, but you cannot.[1]*

1. Quoted in Bill Rockwood, "Interview: Robert Oswald," *Frontline*, November 19, 2013. www.pbs.org/wgbh/pages/frontline/shows/oswald/interviews/oswald.html.

rent and utility bills. He told her that he left as much money as he could to help support her and their child. He also gave her instructions on what to do if he was apprehended after his assassination attempt.

Meanwhile, Oswald was observing Walker through the window of his house. Around 9:00 p.m., Oswald allegedly took a shot at Walker, but he narrowly missed. Oswald returned home, panicky and shaken, and told Marina what he had done. Although he was frightened that he would be arrested, news reports later confirmed that the police had no suspects.

Oswald was not connected to the shooting until after his death and then, only on the basis of testimony by Marina. With no witnesses and no conclusive evidence, there are some who doubt Oswald was involved in the attempted murder of Walker. Conspiracy theorists allege that Marina, as a Russian immigrant, could have easily been pressured by the FBI to incriminate her deceased husband so that he looked more likely to be JFK's assassin. As the Warren report stated, the crime made it appear that Oswald was eager to gain notoriety:

> *[Oswald had] a strong concern for his place in history. If the attack [on Walker] had succeeded and Oswald had been caught, the pictures showing him with his rifle and his Communist ... newspapers would probably have appeared on the front pages of newspapers or magazines all over the country.*[52]

Dangerous Indications

Like many other events tied to the Kennedy assassination, there are a number of different opinions concerning the Walker assassination attempt. However, it is known that Oswald did seem obsessed with getting his name in the papers. Shortly after the Walker shooting, he traveled to New Orleans, where he set up a local branch of the New York City–based Fair Play for Cuba Committee. This organization tried to gather American support for Fidel Castro, the new socialist leader of Cuba. Oswald not only managed the

New Orleans chapter; he was the only member.

Promoting the interests of the Cuban government was considered highly suspect at this time, and Oswald maintained an extremely high profile. He distributed pro-Castro handbills on the street in front of his office. This often provoked loud arguments and even several fistfights. Oswald's activity was photographed several times by the local press. The attention also landed him a spot on a local radio show. During his appearance, Oswald talked intelligently about his interest in Communism, Cuba, and the Soviet Union. In the 1960s, the era of the Cold War, this was almost unheard of in America.

Not even one year after his time in New Orleans, Oswald was accused of plotting and committing the assassination of JFK. Since Oswald's death, he has been called everything from an innocent man to a criminal mastermind. According to Oswald's brother Robert, at the time of the assassination, Oswald's marriage was failing, his dreams of fame were fading, and he was stuck in a dead-end job. With his Marine training, history as a Soviet defector, and mental health problems, Oswald certainly fit the profile of a troubled loner with the means to gain international notoriety.

Many forensic psychologists believe

Oswald's mental instability during his teenage years molded him into a troubled individual who was capable of violence. Looking back, it is clear that "the psychiatric examination of Oswald during adolescence stands as a portrait of his mental state during a critical period of his development."[53] Oswald's psychiatrist at the Youth House, Dr. Hartogs, told the Warren Commission, "I found [Oswald] to have definite traits of dangerousness ... [he] had a potential for explosive, aggressive, assaultive [behavior] which was ...unusual to find in a child."[54]

Though there are thousands of different conspiracy theories about the assassination of JFK, the fact remains that Oswald is the most likely suspect. He had military training, he had a motive to remove Kennedy, and most of all, he was known to have a history of psychological instability. Given the signs of mental health issues observed in his youth, Oswald should have received proper psychiatric treatment, but he did not. If he had, President Kennedy could have been alive on the flight back to the White House on November 22, 1963.

Notes

Chapter One: Assassinating Trust

1. Quoted in House Select Committee on Assassinations, "Findings of the Select Committee on Assassinations in the Assassination of President John F. Kennedy in Dallas, Tex., November 22, 1963," House Select Committee on Assassinations. jfkassassination. net/russ/jfkinfo/hscareport.htm.

2. Quoted in House Select Committee on Assassinations, "Findings of the Select Committee on Assassinations in the Assassination of President John F. Kennedy."

3. Quoted in House Select Committee on Assassinations, "Findings of the Select Committee on Assassinations in the Assassination of President John F. Kennedy."

4. Quoted in Anthony Summers, *Not In Your Lifetime: The Defining Book on the J.F.K Assassination*. New York, NY: Open Road Media, 2013.

5. Quoted in Jim Marrs, *Crossfire: The Plot That Killed Kennedy*. New York, NY: Carroll & Graff, 1989, p. 51.

6. Quoted in Vincent Bugliosi, *Reclaiming History: The Assassination of President John F. Kennedy*. New York, NY: Norton, 2007, p. 106.

7. Quoted in Norman Mailer, *Oswald's Tale: An American Mystery*. New York, NY: Random House, 1995, p. 683.

8. Quoted in Summers, *Not In Your Lifetime*, p. 55.

9. Jim Garrison, *On the Trail of the Assassins*. New York, NY: Warner, 1988, p. 22.

10. Quoted in Summers, *Not In Your Lifetime*, p. 107.

11. Quoted in Richard Belzer, *UFOs, JFK, and Elvis: Conspiracies You Don't Have to Be Crazy to Believe*. New York, NY: Ballantine, 1999, p. 29.

12. Warren Commission, *Report of the Warren Commission on the Assassination of President Kennedy*. New York, NY: McGraw-Hill, 1964, pp. 41–42.

Chapter Two: Doctors and Mysteries

13. Charles A. Crenshaw, *Trauma Room One: The JFK Medical Coverup Exposed*. New York, NY: Paraview, 2001, pp. 67–68.

14. Quoted in Bugliosi, *Reclaiming History*, p. 71.

15. Quoted in Bugliosi, *Reclaiming History*, p. 110.

16. Gerald Posner, *Case Closed: Lee Harvey Oswald and the Assassination of JFK*. New York, NY: Random House, 1993, p. 300.

17. Quoted in House Select Committee on Assassinations, "Testimony of Dr. Cyril H. Wecht, Coroner, Allegheny County, Pa.," House Select Committee on Assassinations. jfkassassination.net/russ/m_j_russ/hscawech.htm.

18. Quoted in Vincent Bugliosi, *Reclaiming History*, p. 1068.

19. Quoted in House Select Committee on Assassinations, "Report of the Select Committee on Assassinations of the U.S. House of Representatives, Section II.—Performance of Autopsy," Kennedy Assassination Home Page. mcadams.posc.mu.edu/autopsy3.txt.

20. Quoted in Belzer, *UFOs, JFK, and Elvis*, p. 35.

Chapter Three: Going Ballistic

21. Mark Lane, *Rush to Judgment*. New York, NY: Thunder's Mouth Press, 1992, p. 149.

22. Quoted in David Miller, *The JFK Conspiracy*. San Jose, CA: Writers Club Press, 2002, p. 157.

23. Quoted in President's Commission on the Assassination of President Kennedy, "Testimony of Robert A. Frazier," The John F. Kennedy Assassination Information Center. mcadams.posc.mu.edu/russ/testimony/frazr1.htm.

24. Quoted in Clint Bradford, "Governor Connally's Wrist Wound and CE-399," JFK Assassination Research Materials, August 1999. www.jfk-info.com/fragment.htm.

25. House Select Committee on Assassinations, "Findings of the Select Committee on Assassinations in the Assassination of President John F. Kennedy."

26. Warren Commission, *Report of the Warren Commission*, p. 104.

Chapter Four: Got It on Tape

27. Quoted in Bugliosi, *Reclaiming History*, p. 377.

28. Quoted in Bugliosi, *Reclaiming History*, p. 377.

29. Quoted in Posner, *Case Closed*, p. 457.

30. Committee on Ballistic Acoustics, National Research Council, "Reexamination of Acoustic Evidence in the Kennedy Assassination," *Science*, October 8, 1982.

31. *LIFE* magazine editors, "A Matter of Reasonable Doubt," *LIFE*, November 22, 1966, p. 41.

32. Warren Commission, *Report of the Warren Commission*, p. 102.

33. Warren Commission, *Report of the Warren Commission*, p. 100.

34. House Select Committee on Assassinations, "Findings of the Select Committee on Assassinations in the Assassination of President John F. Kennedy."

35. Gary L. Aguilar, "The Converging Medical Case for Conspiracy in the Death of JFK," in *Murder in Dealey Plaza*, ed., James H. Fetzer. Chicago, IL: Catfeet Press, 2000, p. 184.

36. Belzer, *UFOs, JFK, and Elvis*, pp. 46–47.

Chapter Five: Exploring Oswald

37. Warren Commission, *Report of the Warren Commission*, p. 351.

38. Quoted in Warren Commission, *Hearings Before the President's Commission on the Assassination of President Kennedy, vol. I.* Washington, DC: Government Printing Office, 1965, p. 225.

39. Quoted in Warren Commission, *Hearings Before the President's Commission on the Assassination of President Kennedy, vol. XI*, Washington, DC: Government Printing Office, 1965, p. 27.

40. Quoted in Warren Commission, *Hearings Before the President's Commission on the Assassination of President Kennedy, vol. VIII*, Washington, DC: Government Printing Office, 1965, p. 103.

41. Evelyn Strickman, "Interview With Boy," Kennedy Assassination Home Page. mcadams.posc.mu.edu/siegel2.htm.

42. Warren Commission, "Testimony of Dr. Renatus Hartogs," Kennedy Assassination Home Page. jfkassassination.net/russ/testimony/hartogs.htm.

43. Charles Patrick Ewing and Joseph T. McCann, *Minds on Trial: Great Cases in Law and Psychology*. New York, NY: Oxford University Press, 2006, p. 24.

44. Quoted in Mailer, *Oswald's Tale*, p. 378.

45. Quoted in Mailer, *Oswald's Tale*, p. 388.

46. Quoted in Bill Rockwood, "Interview: Robert Oswald." *Frontline*, November 19, 2013. www.pbs.org/wgbh/frontline/article/interview-robert-oswald/.

47. Quoted in Gary W. O'Brien, *Oswald's Politics*. Victoria, BC: Trafford, 2010, p. 140.

48. Quoted in Jean Davidson, *Oswald's Game*. New York, NY: Open Road Integrated Media, 1983.

49. Quoted in Rockwood, "Interview: Robert Oswald."

50. Quoted in Bugliosi, *Reclaiming History*, p. 686.

51. Quoted in Edward Jay Epstein, "Question of the Day." edwardjayepstein.com/question_oswald2.htm.

52. Warren Commission, *Report of the Warren Commission*, p. 406.

53. Ewing and McCann, *Minds on Trial*, p. 26.

54. Warren Commission, "Testimony Of Dr. Hartogs."

For More Information

Books

Heiligman, Deborah. *High Hopes: A Photobiography of John F. Kennedy*. Washington, DC: National Geographic, 2003. Using primary source pictures and detailed text, this book covers Kennedy's life from his childhood to his assassination, including events from his administration, such as the Bay of Pigs incident and the Cuban Missile Crisis.

Kurtz, Michael L. *Crime of the Century: The Kennedy Assassination from a Historian's Perspective*. Knoxville, TN: University of Tennessee Press, 2013. This book takes a look at the facts of history that surrounded the murder of President Kennedy, attempting to show readers an honest and open account of the assassination without any political agenda.

Moore, Lance. *Killing JFK: 50 Years, 50 Lies: From the Warren Commission to Bill O'Reilly, a History of Deceit in the Kennedy Assassination*. Lexington, KY: Sky-Fy, 2013. Refuting both conspiracy theories and the official government story, this book boldly tries to assert a new understanding of the Kennedy assassination by looking past the long history of misinformation and manipulated evidence.

Tague, James T. *LBJ and the Kennedy Killing*. Chicago, IL: Trine Day, 2013. Lyndon Johnson, who served as president after Kennedy, is often forgotten in connection with JFK's assassination; this book explores his legacy and how the death of his predecessor impacted his life.

Thomas, Donald Byron. *Hear No Evil: Politics, Science, and the Forensic Evidence in the Kennedy Assassination.* New York, NY: Skyhorse Publishing, 2013.
This book offers an unbiased view that explains both the official story and a number of conspiracy theories regarding the JFK assassination and comes to a conclusion that combines all the facts.

Websites

John F. Kennedy Presidential Library and Museum (www.jfklibrary.org/)
Dedicated to the entirety of President Kennedy's life, this professionally-sourced website gives both a broad and detailed overview of the important moments of his political career, including his assassination.

Kennedy Assassination Home Page (mcadams.posc.mu.edu)
Curated by a professor of history and hosted through Marquette University, this website has articles written by experts in the field, either explaining or refuting theories of the JFK assassination.

"Killing Conspiracy: Why the Best Conspiracy Theories about JFK's Assassination Don't Stand Up to Scrutiny" (www.slate.com/articles/news_ and_politics/history/2013/11/ john_f_kennedy_conspiracy_ theories_debunked_why_the_ magic_bullet_and_grassy.html)
This well-researched article argues against the numerous conspiracy theories surrounding President Kennedy's murder; it also provides links to the numerous sources used to refute many of the theories.

The President John F. Kennedy Assassination Records Collection (www.archives.gov/research/ jfk)
Hosted by the federal government, this website has links to primary sources regarding the murder, including a full

transcription of the Warren Commission's report and the House Select Committee on Assassination's findings.

Who Was Lee Harvey Oswald? (www.pbs.org/wgbh/frontline/film/oswald/)

This PBS website has the full, feature-length *Frontline* program that explores the mysteries surrounding the president's alleged assassin, as well as links to other articles and interviews with key figures in the investigation of Lee Harvey Oswald.

Index

Picture Credits

About the Author

Joseph Stanley is a retired history teacher and baseball coach who lives in a suburb of Buffalo, New York. He has written many books for children and young adults on a wide variety of topics, including several American history books. In addition to writing, he enjoys golfing with his friends and traveling with his wife, children, and grandchildren—with South Carolina and Florida serving as his favorite destinations. He is also an avid sports fan who loves rooting for the Buffalo Bills and New York Yankees.